UK Price
£3.95

AN ILLUSTRATED GUIDE TO

USAF

The Modern US Air Force

a Salamander book

Published by Salamander Books Limited
LONDON

AN ILLUSTRATED GUIDE TO
USAF
The Modern US Air Force

Bill Gunston

A Salamander Book

© 1982 Salamander Books Ltd.,
Salamander House,
27 Old Gloucester Street,
London WC1N 3AF,
United Kingdom.

ISBN 0-86101-136-8

Distributed in the United Kingdom by
New English Library Ltd./
Hodder & Stoughton Ltd.

All correspondence concerning the
content of this volume should be
addressed to Salamander Books Ltd.

Contents

Entries are arranged in alphabetical order of manufacturers' names

Credits

Author: Bill Gunston, former Technical Editor of *Flight Internatonal,* Assistant Compiler of Jane's All The World's Aircraft, contributor to many Salamander illustrated reference books.

Editor: Ray Bonds
Designer: Philip Gorton

Three-view drawings: © Pilot Press Ltd.
Colour profiles: © Pilot Press Ltd., and © Salamander Books Ltd.

Photographs: The publishers wish to thank the United States Air Force for their co-operation in supplying most of the photographs in this book, and also the aircraft manufacturers for their valued assistance

Filmset: by Modern Text Typesetting Ltd.
Printed in Belgium by Henri Proost et Cie.

Introduction

THIS book gives an up-to-date appraisal of the fixed-wing aircraft of today's United States Air Force. It is not concerned with helicopters, which are covered in a companion volume—*An Illustrated Guide to Military Helicopters*—nor with any kind of missile other than those fired or launched from aircraft. ICBMs (intercontinental ballistic missiles) were in the 1950s assigned wholly to the USAF, after a bitter battle in Washington against the Army, and today a significant part of the total Air Force budget goes to the support of Strategic Air Command's Minuteman ICBM force.

For the record, this force is both numerically, and in the size and payload of the missiles, puny compared with the terrifying ICBM capability deployed by the Strategic Rocket Forces of the Soviet Union. While the Soviet rockets have grown in scale, accuracy, numbers and lethality with every week that passes, the USAF has had no funds to buy any *new* missiles at all: the Minuteman force was fully deployed as long ago as April 1967. For many years funds have been provided for a new ICBM, called M-X (Missile-X). Startling amounts have been frittered away on studies of how it could be best deployed so that the missiles would not be destroyed by the Soviet ICBMs.

At the time of writing, spring 1982, the USAF still favours the

Multiple Protective Shelter concept, in which about 200 M-X missiles would be shuttled around a costly network of about 4,600 protective shelters. The only firm decision so far appears to be that this scheme is politically dead. Time and money continue to be used up in studies and arguments, and possibly 50 missiles may from 1986 be put into 50 fixed and therefore vulnerable silos vacated by Titan II missiles which are now being withdrawn from the inventory after 20 years. Details of USAF ICBMs are included among all the world's missiles (from 1916 onwards) in the large Salamander *Encyclopedia of The World's Rockets and Missiles.*

Though the American aerospace industry can in general produce better aircraft and supporting hardware than any other country, and certainly can do it quicker, the price is a severe deterrent to any US administration. Even that of President Reagan, which has been trying to rectify the deferred and negative decisions of the 1970s, has had ▶

Below: As well as aircraft the US Air Force is responsible for the nation's land-based strategic deterrent. For 20 years it has deployed the Minuteman ICBM (salvo launch of two Minuteman III missiles from Vandenberg AFB, right). For 10 years it has searched for a successor, Missile-X (full-scale mock-up, left).

Office of the Secretary of The Air Force

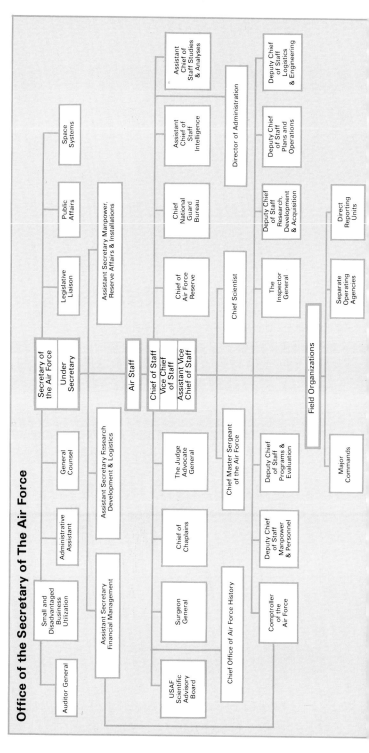

Secretary of the Air Force
Under Secretary

- Auditor General
- Small and Disadvantaged Business Utilization
- Administrative Assistant
- General Counsel
- Legislative Liaison
- Public Affairs
- Space Systems

- Assistant Secretary Financial Management
- Assistant Secretary Research Development & Logistics
- Assistant Secretary Manpower, Reserve Affairs & Installations

Air Staff

Chief of Staff
Vice Chief of Staff
Assistant Vice Chief of Staff

- USAF Scientific Advisory Board
- Surgeon General
- Chief of Chaplains
- The Judge Advocate General
- Chief of Air Force Reserve
- Chief National Guard Bureau
- Assistant Chief of Staff Intelligence
- Assistant Chief of Staff Studies & Analyses

- Chief Office of Air Force History
- Chief Master Sergeant of the Air Force
- Chief Scientist
- The Inspector General
- Director of Administration

- Comptroller of the Air Force
- Deputy Chief of Staff Manpower & Personnel
- Deputy Chief of Staff Programs & Evaluation
- Deputy Chief of Staff Research, Development & Acquisition
- Deputy Chief of Staff Plans and Operations
- Deputy Chief of Staff Logistics & Engineering

Field Organizations

- Major Commands
- Separate Operating Agencies
- Direct Reporting Units

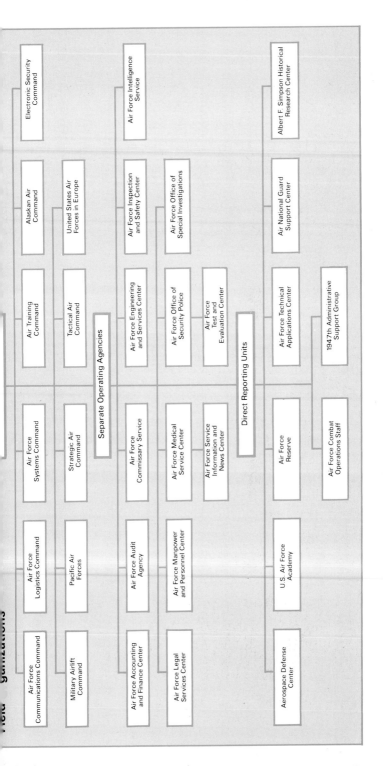

▶to look for ways to cut $13 billion from the defence budget between now and FY84 (Fiscal Year 1984, which ends on 30 June of that year). Several commentators have said that this means actual cuts in 'total obligational authority' of roughly twice this amount, and it means that some major programmes will have to go.

In the quality of its hardware, and the skill, dedication and professionalism of its people, the USAF has never been so good as today, but in its strength to preserve world peace the picture is rather bleak. Abandonment of the nuclear tripwire policy of the 1955-65 era meant that there had to be immensely powerful forces ready to deter aggression anywhere. As these forces have shrunk, so has the President tried to muster a Rapid Deployment Force intended to make a small but effective sharp cutting edge available within 24 hours almost anywhere. Such a force is ill-adapted to counter either the colossal manpower and firepower of the Soviet Union or the religious fanatics and urban terrorists who have chosen to prey upon American lives and property

Below: A 25-year-old KC-135A refuels a B-1 prototype, with an F-15A from 57th Tac Trg Wing in attendance.

Far left: Plans for a Rapid Deployment Force even involve the use of the KC-135 tankers of SAC as carriers of infantry and other ground forces.

Left: This is the best illustration (from Boeing) yet published of the kind of bomber being planned under 'Stealth Technology'.

in recent years. Moreover, for any really large force the USAF would be hard-pressed to provide sufficient airlift. Even if the C-5A did not have to be re-winged, the need for global airlift over intercontinental distances, possibly terminating at austere airstrips, cannot at present be met, and KC-10s and C-17s cannot be procured in anything approaching the necessary numbers.

Apart from a very small force of some 50 FB-111A bombers, the entire winged strength of Strategic Air Command continues to reside in the remaining B-52G and H bombers, plus a few sharply differing B-52Ds, which are now being withdrawn

from the active inventory. The need for a modern long-range deterrent aircraft has been self-evident for 20 years, and the only encouragement that can be drawn from the fact that none has been provided is that today the B-70 (RS-70) would not be the optimum aircraft, just as the B-1 will not be the optimum in 1990. So much time has gone by that any B-1 is better than nothing, and the B-1B, if put into the inventory as at present planned from 1986, will restore credibility to the deterrent that has kept the peace for so long. For the more distant future a 'stealth' bomber has been under study for many years. It has not ▶

Above: Apart from CSIRS (see text below) the costly SR-71 is the only USAF recon platform intended for manned overflights.

▶reached the stage at which it can appear in a book such as this, but in the long term it could be very important indeed, if the US has the will to produce it.

The word 'stealth' has come to mean an aircraft offering minimal signatures to defensive detection systems. Stealth characteristics can be achieved by a combination of aircraft shape, exterior surface quality, materials and several other factors, most importantly the EW (electronic warfare) sub-systems carried on board the aircraft. Surviving in hostile airspace by high flight speed or altitude is no longer viable but, after prolonged effort, stealth technology has reached the point at which it dominates the design of offensive aircraft, not excepting cruise missiles. The USAF is now funding at an increasing rate an ATB (Advanced Tech-

Left: Though the Space Shuttle is a NASA programme—and NASA is careful to maintain its civilian status—the Air Force is certain to be one of the chief customers for operational flights. The OV-102 *Columbia* will open these missions in late 1982, and 74 flights are scheduled in the first four years. Of these approximately 30 per cent of the payload is being booked by the Air Force, which needs Shuttle transportation for a wide range of space activities.

nology Bomber) which it is hoped will supplement the B-1B in the SAC inventory from about 1992. Northrop's appointment as prime contractor generated slightly misleading speculation that the ATB would be a YB-49 type of flying wing. The California company is teamed with Boeing and Vought, with GE providing the vitally important 'zero signature' propulsion.

In the much shorter term Lockheed, which is supplying the TR-1 reconnaissance aircraft designed to non-stealth technology, has for some time been using stealth technology in a relatively small tactical platform called CSIRS (Covert Survivable Inweather Recon/Strike), intended to enter USAF service as early as 1983-4. Using some of the advanced aerodynamics of the SR-71 and GTD-21 RPV, the CSIRS tries to avoid being shot down on multi-sensor reconnaissance and precision attack missions by a combination of high performance and as much stealth technology as could be incorporated in the timescale, for the available budget. It is planned to deploy 20 CSIRS, with possibly more to follow of a more advanced derived type, but the work is largely classified and again could not be included here as a regular USAF type.

At a totally different level, another machine not included is the Piper Enforcer. Unbelievably, ▶

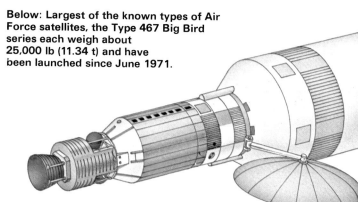

Below: Largest of the known types of Air Force satellites, the Type 467 Big Bird series each weigh about 25,000 lb (11.34 t) and have been launched since June 1971.

▶ this is derived from the P-51 Mustang, first flown to British order in 1940 and subsequently one of the best fighter/bomber aircraft of World War II and the Korean war. During the Vietnam war it often came into discussion, and Cavalier Aircraft sold almost new-build P-51s to the Air Force and Army, though only in small numbers for training and evaluation. Piper, a leading general aviation builder, was asked to produce a largely redesigned Mustang with a turboprop engine to meet a possible need for a light close-support attack aircraft. Piper announced the start of flight testing of the first Enforcer on 29 April 1971, the chosen

engine being the Lycoming T55. Subsequently Piper made no further announcement, and many observers were surprised when in 1981 the company was awarded a three-year contract, for some $2 million, to fly two further Enforcers with many new features. The first is expected to fly at about the time this book appears, but again it can hardly be included in these pages. That there must be a place for a very small, agile, propeller- or fan-engined tactical aircraft, pulling 7g turns at about 300 knots and able to kill tanks and other battlefield targets, appears indisputable. The wisdom of basing it on even a redesigned Mustang

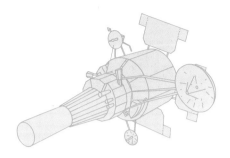

Above: Integrated Missile Early-Warning Satellite uses infra-red sensors to detect ICBM launches.

Left: This NKC-135A has served in different configurations as an airborne laser laboratory.

Below: Though it does not approach the Soviet space effort US surveillance continues: Landsat picture of the Plesetsk Cosmodrome.

is highly questionable.

Today's 'Mustang', of course, is the F-16, and this is perhaps the brightest spot in the entire Air Force inventory. Out of a very limited Light Weight Fighter programme, whose main objective was to see if a useful fighter could be made smaller and cheaper than the F-15, has come a tactical aircraft whose limitations are already hard to probe and are being pushed wider all the time. Perhaps the single event that did most to convert the doubters—whose opinion of the F-16 rested on supposed inadequate avionics, so that it could not do a real job in the bad weather of northern Europe—

was the RAF's annual tac-bombing contest held in mid-1981. A team of seven F-16s from the 388th TFW not only won the contest, beating such specialized attack systems as the Jaguar, Buccaneer and F-111F, but set a remarkable new record in scoring 7,831 of the possible 8,000 points. The USAF can take comfort in the certainty that this aircraft will continue to develop for at least the next 20 years, and will probably be the most numerous aircraft in the inventory for most of that time.

Almost the only shortcoming of the F-16, and it is a shortcoming of every other aeroplane in the USAF, is that it is tied to ▶

▶ airfields whose precise position is known to potential enemies. Those potential enemies having the capability to do so, such as the Soviet Union, could wipe out those bases in minutes. It is simply a matter of everyday fact that, should it choose to do so, the Soviet Union could suddenly and totally destroy every airfield used by all the air forces of NATO, including every operating base of the USAF. It would then be too late to rectify the folly of not deploying strong forces of V/STOL aircraft dispersed so completely through the countryside—if possible at locations offering natural ski jumps—that no amount of satellite recon-

Below: Almost a billion dollars invested in tactical airpower could vanish in a split second if a Soviet ICBM was launched at Langley's 1st Tac Ftr Wing.

naissance could find them, and the task of destroying them by missiles would be uneconomic.

Since 1960 the USAF's position on V/STOL has been variously negative, non-existent and ridiculous. The fact that the only V/STOL actually deployed (in the West) has been of British origin has served to warp and diminish USAF interest in the only survivable form of modern airpower.

Billions spent on B-1B, stealth aircraft and even the agile F-16 will be wasted if at 11 tomorrow morning someone presses a button and sends the whole lot up in fireballs as they stand on their airfield ramps. There would then no longer be any USAF, except perhaps for the planning staffs in the Pentagon and at Air Force Systems Command, who would be left to ponder on where they went wrong . . . .

Beech King Air

VC-6B

Origin: Beech Aircraft Corporation, Wichita, Kansas.
Type: VIP liaison transport.
Engines: Two 580ehp P&WC PT6A-21 turboprops.
Dimensions: Span 50ft 3in (15.32m); length 35ft 6in (10.82m); wing area 293.94sq ft (27.31m²).
Weights: Empty 5,778lb (2.621kg); loaded 9,650lb (4,377kg).
Performance: Maximum cruising speed 256mph (412km/h) at 12,000ft (3,660m); max rate of climb 1,995ft (596m)/min; service ceiling 28,100ft (8,565m); range with max fuel at max cruising speed with allowances, 1,384 miles (2,227km) at 21,000ft (6,400m) at 249mph (401km/h); typical field length, 3,500ft (1,067m).
Armament: None.
History: First flight (company prototype) 20 January 1964; VC-6A delivered to Air Force February 1966.

Development: The Model 90 King Air was essentially a Queen Air fitted with PT6 turboprop engines. With the B90 model the span was increased and gross weight raised considerably to take advantage of the power available. Large numbers of the original A90 series were bought by the Army, for many duties, but a single B90 was bought for the Air Force to serve as a VIP transport--a rare case of a single-aircraft buy of an off-the-shelf type. Originally designated VC-6A, it was later upgraded to VC-6B

Beech Super King Air

C-12A, VC-12A

Origin: Beech Aircraft Corporation, Wichita, Kansas.
Type: Utility, VIP and mixed passenger/cargo transport.
Engines: Two 801ehp P&WC PT6A-38 turboprops.
Dimensions: Span 54ft 6in (16.61m); length 43ft 9in (13.34m); wing area 303sq ft (28.15m²).
Weights: Empty 7,800lb (3,538kg); loaded 12,500lb (5,670kg).
Performance: Maximum cruising speed, 272mph (437km/h) at 30,000ft (9,144m); service ceiling, 31,000ft (9,450m); range at maximum cruising speed, 1,824 miles (2,935km); TO/landing distances, about 2,800ft (850m).
Armament: None.
History: First flight (company prototype) 27 October 1972; first military contract, August 1974.

Development: For many years the top end of the Beechcraft range, and a Cadillac among propeller-driven executive aircraft, the T-tailed Super King Air 200 has found wide acceptance among all the US armed forces. The Air Force purchased 30 of the initial military model, the C-12A, with engines of lower power than commercial and later military variants, resulting in reduced performance. Apart from the lower-powered engines the C-12A was basically an off-the-shelf aircraft for service in various liaison and transport roles. The cockpit is laid out for two-pilot operation, though the right seat may be occupied by a passenger. The main cabin is usually equipped for eight passengers, though other arrangements are in use, and conversion to cargo operation is quick and simple. Avionics are even more comprehensive than usual for a light twin, and provision is made in the baggage area in the rear fuselage for storing survival gear. The interior is fully pressurized and air-conditioned, and the wing and tail are deiced by

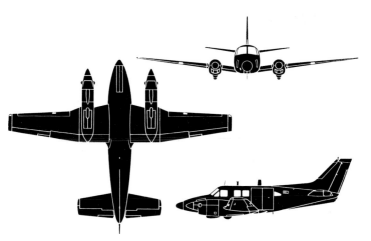

Above: The Beech VC-6B is a USAF B90 (now C90) with small changes.

standard with small modifications. Tail number is 66-7943 and the aircraft serves with the 89th Military Airlift Group at Andrews AFB, near Washington, DC, as a unit of the 1254th Special Air Missions Squadron. Unlike previous King Air models the B90 is pressurized, and of course the VC-6B is fully equipped for flight in bad weather, by night or in severe icing conditions.

Above: A USAF VC-12A in company with a US Army C12-A Huron (rear). Both are variants of pressurised Super King Air.

pneumatic boots. Aircraft styled VC-12A are equipped for VIP duties, with the 89th Military Airlift Group at Andrews AFB, Maryland, adjacent to DC. Other C-12As are assigned to overseas HQs or embassies; for example at Ramstein AB, HQ of USAFE.

Beech has always been the top General Aviation company for military contracts. It has played a major role in missile and space programmes, and is also one of the largest producers of RPVs (remotely piloted vehicles) and target drones, current types including the Mach 3 AQM-37A and MQM-107 Streaker family. Beech also makes airframes for Bell OH-58 Kiowa and JetRanger helicopters and portions of UH-1 Iroquois helicopters under subcontract to Bell Helicopter Textron.

Boeing B-52 Stratofortress

B-52D, G and H

Origin: Boeing Airplane Company (from May 1961 The Boeing Company), Seattle, Washington.

Type: Heavy bomber and missile platform.

Engines: (D) eight 12,100lb (5,489kg) thrust P&WA J57-19W or 29W turbojets, (G) eight 13,750lb (6,237kg) thrust P&WA J57-43W or -43WB turbojets, (H) eight 17,000lb (7,711kg) thrust P&WA TF33-1 or -3 turbofans.

Dimensions: Span 185ft 0in (56.39m); length (D, and G/H as built) 157ft 7in (48.0m), (G/H modified) 160ft 11in (49.05m); height (D) 48ft 4½in (14.7m), (G/H) 40ft 8in (12.4m); wing area 4,000sq ft (371.6m²).

Weights: Empty (D) about 175,000lb (79,380kg), (G/H) about 195,000lb (88,450kg); loaded (D) about 470,000lb (213,200kg), (G) 505,000lb (229,000kg), (H) 505,000 at takeoff, inflight refuel to 566,000lb (256,738kg).

Performance: Maximum speed (true airspeed, clean), (D) 575mph (925km/h), (G/H) 595mph (957km/h); penetration speed at low altitude (all) about 405mph (652km/h, Mach 0.53); service ceiling (D) 45,000ft (13.7km), (G) 46,000ft (14.0km), (H) 47,000ft (14.3km); range (max fuel, no external bombs/missiles, optimum hi-alt cruise) (D) 7,370 miles (11,861km), (G) 8,406 miles (13,528km), (H) 10,130 iles (16,303km); takeoff run, (D) 11,100ft (3,383m), (G) 10,000ft (3,050m), (H) 9,500ft (2895m).

Armament: (D) four 0.5in (12.7mm) guns in occupied tail turret, MD-9 system, plus 84 bombs of nominal 500lb (227kg) in bomb bay plus 24 of nominal 750lb (340kg) on wing pylons, total 60,000lb (27,215kg); (G) four 0.5in (12.7mm) guns in remote-control tail turret, ASG-15 system, plus 8 nuclear bombs or up to 20 SRAM, ALCM or mix (eight on internal dispenser plus 12 on wing plyons); (H) single 20mm six-barrel gun in remote-control tail turret, ASG-21 system, plus bombload as G.

History: First flight 15 April 1952; later, see text.

Above: B-52H No 60-0062 was used for SRAM compatibility testing.

Development: Destined to be the longest-lived aircraft in all aviation history, the B-52 was designed to the very limits of the state of the art in 1948-49 to meet the demands of SAC for a long-range bomber and yet achieve the high performance possible with jet propulsion. The two prototypes had tandem pilot positions and were notable for their great size and fuel capacity, four double engine pods and four twin-wheel landing ▶

Left: The B-52G is not only the most numerous of all B-52 variants but also the most consistently updated model. At present it is the only sub-type to be armed with the AGM-86B cruise missile.

Below: The monster drag chute, usually of 32ft (9.75m) size, is not often used. This aircraft is a B-52H, photographed in 1981 with all avionic updates including ALQ-153 on the fin.

▶ trucks which could be slewed to crab the aircraft on to the runway in a crosswind landing. The B-52A changed to a side-by-side pilot cockpit in the nose and entered service in August 1954, becoming operational in June 1955. Subsequently 744 aircraft were built in eight major types, all of which have been withdrawn except the B-52D, G and H.

The B-52D fleet numbered 170 (55-068/-117, 56-580/-630 built at Seattle and 55-049/-067, 55-673/-680 and 56-657/-698 built at Wichita) delivered at 20 per month alongside the same rate for KC-135 tankers in support. The B-52G was the most numerous variant, 193 being delivered from early 1959 (57-6468/-6520, 58-158/-258 and 59-2564/-2602, all from Wichita), introducing a wet (integral-tank) wing which increased internal fuel from 35,550 to 46,575 US gal and also featured shaft-driven ▶

Top: B-52G No. 59-2565 in the current colour scheme.

Right: Totally unlike the cockpits of early versions, the B-52G and H flight decks are dominated by EVS (TV and infra-red) displays.

Below: These B-52H bombers are the newest of the entire family, already at more than double the original design structure life.

▶generators, roll control by spoilers only, powered tail controls, injection water in the leading edge, a short vertical tail, rear gunner moved to the main pressurized crew compartment and an inner wing stressed for a large pylon on each side. The final model, the B-52H, numbered 102 (60-001/-062 and 61-001/-040), and was essentially a G with the new TF33 fan engine and a new tail gun.

During the Vietnam war the B-52D was structurally rebuilt for HDB (high-density bombing) with conventional bombs, never considered in the original design. The wings were given inboard pylons of great length for four tandem triplets of bombs on each side, and as noted in the data 108 bombs could be carried in all with a true weight not the 'book value' given but closer to 89,100lb (40,400kg). Another far-reaching and costly series of structural modifications was needed on all models to permit sustained operations at low level, to keep as far as possible under hostile radars, again not previously considered. The newest models, the G and H were given a stability▶

Right: Newest of the B-52s, the B-52H combines the high-capacity wet wing of the B-52G with the economical TF33 turbofan engine.

Below: Aircrews 'scramble' toward a line-up of G models during the 1979 Global Shield exercises.

Above: A live drop of a SRAM from a B-52H, showing the point of maximum fall at which the first-pulse rocket motor ignites.

Above: A live drop of an AGM-86A cruise missile, from a special test NB-52G in 1976. The production ALCM is longer.

Below: Taken in May 1979, this picture shows one of the B-52Gs used for the fly-off ALCM competition; the AGM-86Bs are dummies.

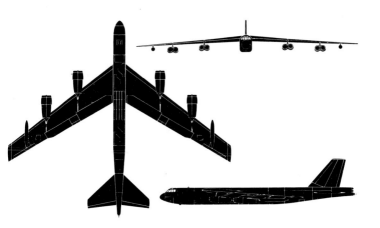

Above: Three-view of Boeing B-52H, without EVS blisters.

augmentation system from 1969 to improve comfort and airframe life in turbulent dense air. From 1972 these aircraft were outfitted to carry the SRAM (Short-Range Attack Missile), some 1,300 of which are still with the SAC Bomb Wings. Next came the EVS (Electro-optical Viewing System) which added twin chin bulges. The Phase VI ECM (electronic counter-measures) cost $362.5 million from 1973. Quick Start added cartridge engine starters to the G and H for a quick getaway to escape missile attack. Next came a new threat-warning system, a satellite link and 'smart noise' jammers to thwart enemy radars. From 1980 the venerable D-force was updated by a $126.3 million digital nav/bombing system. Further major changes to the G and H include the OAS (offensive avionics system) which is now in progress costing $1,662 million. The equally big CMI (cruise-missile interface) will eventually fit the G-force for 12 AGM-86B missiles on the pylons, the first 16 aircraft being scheduled to become operational in December 1982. Later the bomb bays will be rebuilt to carry this missile, and eventually AGM-86B may also go into the H-fleet.

Altogether about 340 B-52s remain in SAC's active inventory, 70 being conventional-bomb D-models and 270 the very different and more sophisticated G and H. These equip 17 Bomb Wings all with home bases in the Continental US. A further 187 aircraft are in storage.

Boeing C-135 family

Origin: Boeing Airplane Company (from May 1961 The Boeing Company), Seattle, Washington.
Type: Tankers, transports, EW, Elint, command-post and rsearch aircraft.
Engines: (A and derivatives) four 13,750lb (6,273kg) thrust P&WA J57-59W or -43WB turbojets, (B and derivatives) four 18,000lb (8165kg) thrust P&WA TF33-3 turbofans, (RE) four 22,000lb (9,979kg) thrust CFM56-1B11 turbofans.
Dimensions: Span (basic) 130ft 10in (39.88m); length (basic) 134ft 6in (40.99m); height (basic) 38ft 4in (11.68m), (tall fin) 41ft 8in (12.69m; wing area 2,433sq ft (226m²).
Weights: empty (KC-135A basic) 98,466lb (44,664kg), (KC, operating weight) 106,306lb (48,220kg), (C-135B) 102,300lb (46,403kg); loaded (KC, original) 297,000lb (134,719kg), (KC, later max) 316,000lb (143,338kg), (C-135B) 275,000lb (124,740kg) (typical of special variants).
Performance: Maximum speed (all) about 580mph (933km/h); typical high-speed cruise, 532mph (856km/h) at 35,000ft (10.7km); initial climb (J57, typical) 1,290ft (393m)/min, (TF33) 4,900ft (1,494m)/min; service ceiling (KC, full load) 36,000ft (10.9km), (C-135B) 44,000ft (13.4km); mission radius (KC) 3,450 miles (5,552km) to offload 24,000lb (10,886kg) transfer fuel, 1,150 miles (1,950km) to offload 120,000lb (54,432kg); field length (KC, ISA+17°C) 13,700ft (4,176m).
Armament: None.
History: First flight 31 August 1956, variants see text.

Development: Boeing risked more than the company's net worth to build a prototype jetliner, first flown in July 1954. An important factor behind the gamble was the belief the USAF would buy a jet tanker/transport to replace the Boeing KC-97 family, and this belief was justified by the announcement of an initial order for 29 only three weeks after the company prototype flew, and long before it had done any inflight refuelling tests. The KC-135A Stratotanker differed only in minor respects from the original prototype, whereas the civil 707 developed in a parellel programme was a totally fresh design with a wider fuselage, airframe of 2024 alloy designed on fail-safe principles and totally revised systems. The KC-135A was thus a rapid programme and deliveries began on 30 April 1957, building up to a frantic 20 per month and eventually reaching 732 aircraft. ▶

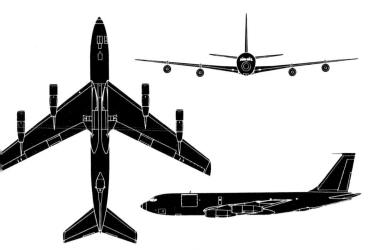

Above: Three-view of KC-135B (TF33 turbofan engines).

Above: The EC-135C (14 aircraft) are airborne command posts used by SAC to command all deterrent operations backing up the E-4 fleet. Powered by fan engines and retaining the boom, they have blade, wire, saddle and ventral trailing-wire aerials, plus HF probes on the wingtips.

Left: The 1956-built third KC-135 seen in the 1960s as a KC-135R, with rebuilt front and rear fuselage. In 1971 it became the sole RC-135T.

▶ The basic KC-135A has a windowless main fuselage with 80 tip-up troop or ground-crew seats and a cargo floor with tiedown fittings. Fuel is carried in 12 wing tanks and nine in the fuselage, only one of the latter being above the main floor (at the extreme tail). All but 1,000 US gal (3,785 lit) may be used as transfer fuel, pumped out via a Boeing high-speed extensible boom steered by a boom operator lying prone in the bottom of the rear fuselage. Only one receiver aircraft can be refuelled at a time, keeping station by watching rows of lights along the underside of the forward fuselage. The original short fin was later superseded by a tall fin and powered rudder, and many tankers were given an ARR (air refuelling receiver) boom receptacle. The KC force numbers 615 active aircraft in 35 squadrons, including 80 aircraft in Reserve units. The 100th ARW (Air Refueling Wing) at Beale AFB exclusively uses the KC-135Q with special avionics and JP-7 fuel for the SR-71 aircraft.

MATS, now MAC, bought 15 C-135A and 30 C-135B Stratolifter transports, the Bs with fan engines with reversers and much sprightlier performance with less noise and smoke. These remained windowless but had the refuelling boom removed (though retaining the operator's blister) and were equipped for 126 troops or 89,000lb (40,370kg) cargo loaded through a large door forward on the left side. In MATS these aircraft were soon replaced by the C-141. The final new-build versions were the four RC-135A survey/mapping aircraft for MATS and ten RC-135B for strategic reconnaissance. Thus, total C-135 production for the USAF numbered 808, completed in February 1965.

Since then the family has swelled by modification to become perhaps the most diverse in aviation history, the following all being USAF variants: EC-135A, radio link (SAC post-attack command control system); EC-135B, AF Systems Command, ex-RIA (Range Instrumented Aircraft) mainly twice-rebuilt; EC-135C, SAC command posts; EC-135G, ICBM launch and radio link (with boom); EC-135H, airborne command posts; EC-135J, airborne command posts (Pacaf); EC-135K, airborne command posts (TAC); EC-135L, special SAC relay platforms; EC-135N, now C-135N, Apollo range, four with A-LOTS pod tracker; EC-135P, communications/command posts; KC-135A, original designation retained for SAC relay links; KC-135R, also RC-135R, special recon/EW rebuilds; NC-135A, USAF, NASA and AEC above-ground nuclear-test and other radiation studies; NKC-135A, Systems Command fleet for ECM/ECCM, laser, ionosphere, missile vulnerability, icing, comsat, weightless, boom and other research; RC-135B and C, recon aircraft with SLAR cheeks and other sensors; RC-135D, different SLARs and thimble noses; RC-135E, glassfibre forward fuselage and inboard wing pods; RC-135M, numerous electronic installations, fan engines; RC-135S,

Below: A standard KC-135A refuels two F-4Es and an F-4D over SE Asia. It has the tall fin and powered rudder (a modification).

Above: This RC-135V is unlike most of the seven of this type in having HF wingtip probes as well as SLAR cheeks and ventral blades.

Above: The HF probes above the wingtips show clearly on this EC-135J of Pacaf, as well as the black saddle dome.

most M installations plus many others; RC-135T, single special SAC aircraft; RC-135U, special sensors and aerials cover almost entire airframe, including SLAR cheeks, extended tailcone and various chin, dorsal, ventral and fin aerials; RC-135V, rebuild of seven Cs and one U with nose thimble, wire aerials and ventral blades; RC-135W, latest recon model mostly rebuilt from M with SLAR sheeks added; WC-135B, standard MAC weather platforms.

Below: One of the 56 tankers modified to KC-135Q configuration, with special provisions for JP-7 (SR-71) fuel and grey Corogard finish.

Boeing VC-137

VC-137B, C

Origin: The Boeing Company, Seattle, Washington.
Type: Special missions transport.
Engines: Four 18,000lb (8,165kg) thrust P&WA JT3D-3 turbofans.
Dimensions: Span (B) 130ft 10in (39.87m); (C) 145ft 9in (44.42m); length (B) 144ft 6in (44.04m), (C) 152ft 11in (46.61m); wing area (B) 2,433sq ft (226m²), (C) 3,010sq ft (279.64m²).
Weights: Empty (B) about 124,000lb (56,250kg), (C) about 140,500lb (63,730kg); loaded (B) 258,000lb (117,025kg), (C)322,000lb (146,059kg).
Performance: Maximum speed (B) 623mph (1002km/h), (C) 627mph (1010km/h); maximum cruise, (B) 618mph (995km/h) (C) 600mph (966km/h); initial climb (B) 5,050ft (1539m)/min, (C) 3,550ft (1,082m)/min; service ceiling (B) 42,000ft (12.8km), (C) 38,500ft (11.73km); range, maximum payload, (B) 4,235 miles (6,820km), (C), 6,160 miles (9915km).
Armament: None.
History: First flight (civil-120B) 22 June 1960, (-320B) 31 January 1962.

Development: These aircraft bear no direct relationship to the prolific C135 family but were commercial airliners (hence the civil engine designation) bought off-the-shelf but specially furnished for the MAC 89th Military Airlift Group, based at Andrews AFB, Maryland, to fly the President and other senior executive officials. All have rear cabins with regular airline seating but

---

Boeing T-43

T-43A

Origin: The Boeing Company, Seattle, Washington.
Type: Navigator trainer.
Engines: Two 14,500lb (6,577kg) thrust P&WA JT8D-9 turbofans.
Dimensions: Span 93ft 0in (28.35m); length 100ft 0in (30.48m); wing area 980 sq ft (91.05m²).
Weights: Empty 64,090lb (29,071kg); loaded 115,500lb (52,391kg).
Performance: Maximum cruising speed 562mph (904km/h); normal cruising speed, about 464mph (747km/h) at 35,000ft (10.67km); range with MIL-C-5011A reserves, 2,995 miles (4,820km).
Armament: None.
History: First flight (737-100) 9 April 1967, (T-43A) 10 April 1973.

Development: Vietnam experience revealed a serious deficiency of facilities for training modern navigators, the only aircraft for this purpose being 77 T-29 piston-engined machines based on the immediate post-war Convair-Liner. In May 1971 the Air Force announced an $87.1 million order for 19 off-the-shelf Boeing 737-200s, with an option (not taken up) for a further ten. The 19 aircraft were delivered in the 12 months from June 1973, and all have since operated with the 323rd Flying Training Wing at Mather AFB, California. Numerous change orders were issued to the basic 737-200, though engines and equipment items are treated as commercial (there is no military designation for the JT8D). There is only a single door and nine windows along each side of the cabin, the floor is strengthened to carry heavy avionics consoles and operating desks, there are additional avionics aerials, and an 800 US-gal (3027 lit) auxiliary fuel tank is installed in the aft cargo compartment. In addition to the two pilots and supernumerary there are stations for 12 pupil navigators, four advanced trainees and three instructors. Training is given under all weather conditions and at all heights, with equipment which is often modified to reflect that in operational types.

32

Above: Air Force One is strictly so-called only when the US President is aboard; at all other times it is just an immaculately polished VC-137C which uses regular USAF callsigns.

a special midships HQ/conference section and a forward communications centre with special avionics in contact with stations on land, sea, in the air and in space. There are special security provisions. The two VC-137Bs were bought as early 707-153s with JT3C-6 engines and were redesignated on fitting turbofan engines. The first VC-137CC (62-6000), a much larger aircraft equivalent to a 707-320B, was the original Presidential Air Force One. It is now back-up to today's Air Force One, 72-7000.

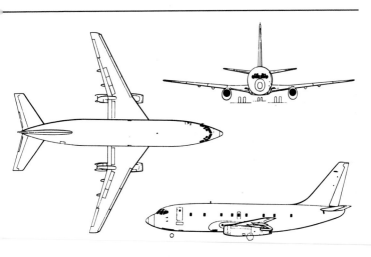

Above: Standard configuration of the T-43A.

Below: All specialist USAF navigators have trained on the T-43A.

Boeing E-3 Sentry

E-3A

Origin: Boeing Aerospace Company, Kent, Washington.
Type: Airborne Warning and Control System (AWACS) platform.
Engines: Four 21,000lb (952kg) thrust P&WA TF33-100/100A turbofans.
Dimensions: Span 145ft 9in (44,42m); length 152ft 11in (46.61m); height 41ft 4in (12.6m) (over fin); wing area 3,050sq ft (283.4m²).
Weights: Empty, not disclosed but about 162,000lb (73,480kg), loaded 325,00lb (147,400kg).
Performance: Maximum speed 530mph (853km/h); normal operating speed, about 350mph (563km/h); service ceiling, over 29,000ft (8.85km); endurance on station 1,000 miles (1,609km) from base, 6h.
Armament: None.
History: First flight (EC-137D) 5 February 1972, (E-3A) 31 October 1975; service delivery (E-3A) 24 March 1977.

Development: The USAF had been one of the pioneers of overland surveillance platforms, mainly using EC-121 Warning Stars (based on the Super Constellation, and continuing in unpublicized service until almost 1980). During the 1960s radar technology had reached the point at which, with greater power and rapid digital processing, an OTH (over the horizon) capability could be achieved, plus clear vision looking almost straight down to detect and follow high-speed aircraft flying only just above the Earth's surface. One vital ingredient was the pulse-doppler kind of radar, in which ▶

Right: The first flight-cleared Westinghouse APY-1 radar was tested in this EC-137D (converted 707).

Below: Another photograph of the original EC-137D which from 1972 completed most of the AWACS test programme with the exception of inflight refuelling.

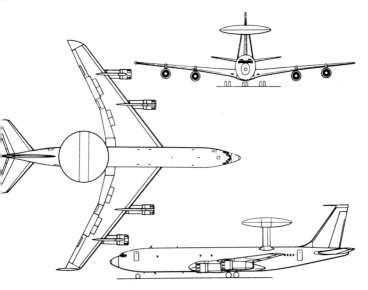

Above: Three view of the production E-3A (rotodome parked).

▶the 'doppler shift' in received frequency caused by relative motion between the target and the radar can be used to separate out all reflections except those from genuine moving targets. Very clever signal processing is needed to eliminate returns from such false 'moving targets' as leaves violently distributed by wind, and the most difficult of all is the motion of the sea surface and blown spray in an ocean gale. For this reason even more clever radars are needed for the overwater mission, and the USAF did not attempt to accomplish it until quite recently. ▶

**Right: Takeoff of an EC-137D test aircraft, with rotodome revolving.
Below: E-3A Sentries of the USAF 963rd AWAC Squadron at
Tinker AFB, Oklahoma. This is a unit of the 552nd AWAC Wing of TAC.**

37

► While Hughes and Westinghouse fought to develop the new ODR (overland downlock radar), Boeing was awarded a prime contract on 8 July 1970 for the AWACS (Airborne Warning And Control System). Their proposal was based on the commercial 707-320; to give enhanced on-station endurance it was to be powered by eight TF34 engines, but to cut costs this was abandoned and the original engines retained thought driving high-power electric generators. The aerial for the main radar, back-to-back with an IFF (identification friend or foe) aerial and communications aerials, is mounted on a pylon above the rear fuselage and streamlined by adding two D-shaped radomes of glassfibre sandwich which turn the girdler-like aerial array into a deep circular rotordome of 30ft (9.14m) diameter. This turns very slowly to keep the bearings lubricated; when on-station it rotates at 6rpm (once every ten seconds) and the searchlight-like beam is electronically scanned under computer control to sweep from the ground up to the sky and space, picking out every kind of moving target and processing the resulting signals at the rate of 710,000 complete 'words' per second. The rival radars were flown in two EC-137D aircraft rebuilt from existing 707s, and the winning Westinghouse APY-1 radar was built into the first E-3A in 1975. The first E-3A force was built up in TAC, to support quick-reaction deployment and tactical operation by all TAC units. The 552nd AWAC Wing received its first E-3A at Tinker AFB, Oklahoma, on 24 March 1977, and went on operational duty a year later. Subsequently the 552nd have operated in many parts of the world. It was augmented from 1979 by NORAD (North American Air Defense) personnel whose mission is the surveillance of all North American airspace and the control of NORAD forces over the Continental USA.

From the 22nd aircraft in 1981 an overwater capability has been incorporated, and from No 24 the systems are to an upgraded standard linked into the JTIDS (Joint TActical Information Distribution System) shared by all US services as well as NATO forces which use 18 similar aircraft. The planned USAF force is 34 aircraft, funded at two per year and due to be complete in 1985.

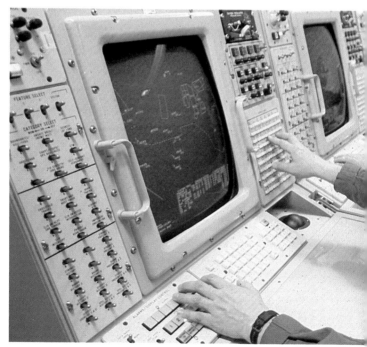

Above: A recent portrait of an E-3A Sentry of the TAC 552nd AWAC Wing, taken from the boomer's position of a KC-135A tanker. The Sentry's inflight-refuelling receptacle can be seen open, ready to receive the high-speed boom of the tanker. Normal endurance on station 1,000 miles (1,610km) from base is six hours, without an inflight refuelling.

Left: Of a normal complement of 17, only four are needed to fly the E-3A. The rest are AWACS specialists; their number can vary between about 12 and 15 according to the demands of the mission and tactical situation. Most, including those pictured, sit at MPCs (multi-purpose consoles), nine of which are installed in the standard AWACS configuration, along with two auxiliary displays.

Boeing E-4 AABNCP

E-4B

Origin: Boeing Aerospace Company, Kent, Washington.
Type: Advanced airborne command post.
Engines: Four 52,500lb (23,814kg) thrust General Electric F103-100 turbofans.
Dimensions: Span 195ft 8in (59.64m); length 231ft 10in (70.66m); wing area 5,500 sq ft (511m²).
Weights: Empty, not disclosed but about 410,000lb (186 tonnes); loaded 820,000lb (371,945kg).
Performance: Maximum speed, 700,000lb (317,515kg) at 30,000ft (9,144m), 602mph (969km/h); typical cruising speed, 583mph (939km/h) at 35,000ft (10,670m); maximum range with full tanks, 7,100 miles (11,426km); takeoff field length, ISA, 10,400ft (317m); cruise ceiling, 45,000ft (13,715m).
Armament: None.
History: First flight (747 prototype) 9 February 1969, (E-4A) 13 June 1973.

Development: This unique variant of the commercial 747 transport is being procured in small numbers to replace the various EC-135 airborne command posts of the US National Military Command System and SAC. ▶

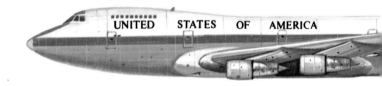

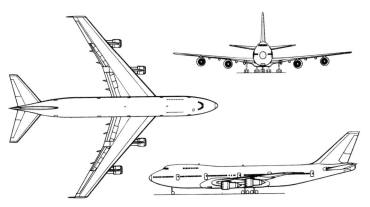

Above: Three-view of original E-4A with F105 (JT9D) engines.

Left: This profile depicts the first 747 to be brought up to E-4A standard, with Pratt & Whitney F105 (JT9D) engines. The same aircraft, USAF 75-0125, is shown overleaf completely updated to E-4B standard.

Below: A production E-4A, USAF 80-1676, operating with SAC prior to being brought up to E-4B standard. These aircraft have the same livery as Air Force One.

▶Under the 481B AABNCP (Advanced Airborne National Command Post) programme the Air Force Electronic Systems Division awarded Boeing a contract in February 1973 for the first two unequipped aircraft, designated E-4A and powered by JT9D engines, to which a third aircraft was added in July 1973. E-Systems won the contract to instal interim equipment in these three E-4A aircraft, the first of which was delivered to Andrews AFB in December 1974. The next two were delivered in 1975.

The third E-4A differed in being powered by the GE F103 engine, and this was made standard and subsequently retrofitted to the first two aircraft in December 1973 a fourth aircraft was contracted for, and this was fitted with more advanced equipment resulting in the designation E-4B. All AABNCP aircraft have been brought up to the same standard and are designated E-4B. The first E-4B (75-0125), the fourth in the E-4 series, was delivered on 21 December 1979. The E-4B has accommodation for a larger battle staff on its 4,620 sq ft (429.2m²) main deck, which is divided into six operating areas: the National Command Authorities area, conference room briefing room, battle staff, communications control centre and rest area. The flight deck includes a special navigation station (not in 747s) and crew rest area,

Above: Takeoff of 80-1676 in original E-4A configuration.

The first E-4B, 75-0125 after further reconstruction, was redelivered to the Air Force in December 1979. It has the SHF 'doghouse' communications blister.

essential for air-refuelled missions lasting up to 72 hours. Lobe areas under the main deck house technical controls and stores for on-board maintenance.

One of the world's most costly military aircraft types, the E-4B is designed for unique capabilities. Its extraordinary avionics, mainly communications but including many other types of system, were created by a team including Electrospace Systems, Collins, Rockwell, RCA and Burroughes, co-ordinated by E-Systems and Boeing. Each engine drives two 150kVA alternators, and a large air-conditioning system (separate from that for the main cabin) is provided to cool the avionics compartments. Nuclear thermal shielding is extensive, and among the communications are an LF/VLF using a wire aerial trailed several miles behind the aircraft, and an SHF (super high frequency) system whose aerials are housed in the dorsal blister that was absent from the E-4A. Since November 1975 the sole operational management for the AABNCP force has been vested in SAC, and the main base is Offutt AFB, Nebraska. This is home to the 55th Strategic Recon Wing, user of the EC-135 command posts, but it has not been announced whether the E-4Bs are also assigned to this wing. Planned force is six aircraft, five of which were in use in 1982.

Above: Inflight refuelling of an E-4A (probably 0125).

Cessna O-2 Skymaster

Model 337, O-2A

Origin: Cessna Aircraft Company, Wichita, Kansas.
Type: Forward air control and reconnaissance.
Engines: Tandem 210hp Continental IO-360C six-cylinder.
Dimensions: Span 38ft 2in (11.63m); length 29ft 9in (9.07m); wing area 202.5sq ft (18.8m²).
Weights: Empty 2,848lb (11,292kg); loaded (max) 5,400lb (2,448kg).
Performance: Maximum speed 200mph (322km/h); cruising speed 144mph (232km/h); initial climb 1,180ft (360m)/min; service ceiling 18,000ft (5,490m); takeoff or landing over 50ft (15m), 1,675ft (510m); range with max fuel, 1,325 miles (2,132km).
Armament: Can carry underwing 7.62mm Minigun pod, light rockets or other light ordnance.
History: First flight (337 prototype) 28 February 1961, (O-2A) early 1967.

Development: The USAF placed a contract with Cessna for a military version of the Model 337 Skymaster 'push/pull' twin to supplement and then replace the single-engined O-1. Features included side-by-side dual controls for pilot and observer (the latter having extra windows low on the right side), four underwing pylons for flares or many other loads, and extensive navaids and communications systems. By 1971 a total of over 350 had been delivered, plus some 160 O-2B spy-war aircraft. Today large numbers of O-2A serve in utility and FAC rfoles with TAC's 24th CW at Howard AFB, Canal Zone, 507th TACW at Shaw AFB, SC, and 602nd TACW at Bergstrom, Texas; USAFE's 601st TCW at Sembach; Alaska's 25th TASS at Eielson AFB; and in the following ANG units: 105th TASW, White Plains, NY; 110th TASG, Battle Creek, Mich; 111th TASG, Willow Grove, Pa; 115th TASW, Traux Field, Wis; 163rd TASG, Ontario, Calif; and 182nd TASG, Peoria, Ill.

Cessna T-41

Model 172, T-41A Mescalero, T-41C.

Origin: Cessna Aircraft Company, Wichita, Kansas.
Type: Primary pilot trainer.
Engine: (A) one 150hp Lycoming O-320-E2D, (C) 210hp Continental IO-360-D.
Weights: Empty (A) 1,363lb (618kg); loaded (A) 2,300lb (1,043kg).
Performance: Maximum speed (A) 144mph (232km/h), (C) 153mph (246km/h); maximu mcruising speed (A) 138mph (22km/h), (C) 145mph (233km/h); initial climb (A) 645ft (196m)/min, (C) 880ft (268m)/min; service ceiling (A) 13,100ft (3,995m), (C) 17,000ft (5,180m).
Armament: None
History: First flight (civil 172) 1955, (T-41A) August 1964.

Development: The high cost of pupil wastage (failure) in all-jet training prompted the Air Force to reconsider its policy, and in July 1964, after two years of study, the decision was taken to introduce a light piston-engined machine for initial training, to weed out pupils with an initial 30h at relatively low cost. The Model 172 was picked off-the-shelf, and 170 were ordered as the T-41A Mescalero, total orders to date being 237 (the last in 1973). Joint civil/military serials are carried, without national insignia, and the USAF aircraft are operated by eight civilian contract schools located near USAF undergraduate pilot schools. In addition 52 more powerful T-41Cs were purchased for cadet training at the Air Force Academy at Colorado Springs. These resemble the civil 172E but have fixed-pitch propellers.

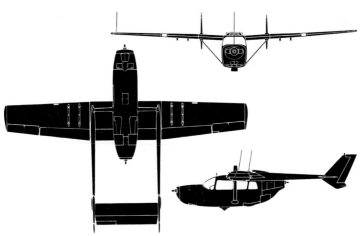

Above: Three-view of standard Cessna O-2A.

Below: The first of the 160 O-2B psychological-warfare aircraft.

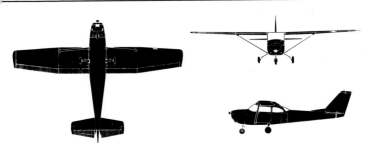

Above: Three-view of standard T-41A Mescalero.

Below: The civil and USAF numbers are repetitive.

Cessna T-37

Model 318, T-37B, A-37B Dragonfly

Origin: Cessna Aircraft Company, Wichita, Kansas.
Type: T-37, primary trainer; A-37, light attack.
Engines: (T) two 1,025lb (465kg) thrust Teledyne CAE J69-25 turbojets, (A) two 2,850lb (1293kg) thrust General Electric J85-17A turbojets.
Dimensions: Span (T) 33ft 9.3in (10.3m), (A, over tanks) 35ft 10.5in (10.93m); length (T) 29ft 3in (8.92m), (A, excl refuelling probe) 28ft 3.25in (8.62m); wing area 183.9 sq ft (17.09m²).
Weights: Empty (T) 3,870lb (1,755kg), (A) 6,211lb (2,817kg); loaded (T) 6,600lb (2,993kg) (A) 14,000lb (6,350kg).
Performance: Maximum speed (T) 426mph (685km/h), (A) 507mph (816km/h); normal cruising speed (T) 380mph (612km/h), (A, clean) 489mph (787km/h); initial climb (T) 3,020ft (920m)/min, (A) 6,990ft (2130m)/min; service ceiling (T) 35,100ft (10,700m), (A) 41,765ft (12,730m); range (T, 5% reserves, 25,000ft/7,620m cruise) 604 miles (972km), (A, max fuel, four drop tanks) 1,012 miles (1628km), (A, max payload including 4,100lb/1860kg ordnance) 460 miles (740km).
Armament: (T) None, (A) GAU-2B/A7.62mm Minigun in fuselage, eight underwing pylons (four inners 870lb/394kg each, next 600lb/272kg and outers 500lb/227kg) for large number of weapons, pods, dispensers, clusters, launchers or recon/EW equipment.
History: First flight (T) 12 October 1954, (A) 22 October 1963. ▶

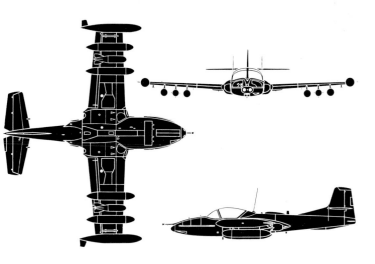

Above: Three-view of A-37B Dragonfly with bombs and tanks.

Left: As described overleaf, the A-37B equips squadrons in both the AF Reserve and the Air National Guard. It is an excellent low-cost attack training type.

Below: Though the A-37B (rear) is twice as heavy as the T-37A (foreground) its more powerful engines give it a somewhat better flight performance.

▶**Development:** After prolonged study the Air Force decided in 1952 to adopt a jet primary pilot trainer, and after a design competition the Cessna Model 318 was selected. Features included all-metal stressed-skin construction, side-by-side seating in a cockpit with ejection seats and a single broad clamshell canopy, two small engines in the wing roots with nozzles at the trailing edge, fixed tailplane half-way up the fin, manual controls with electric trim, hydraulic slotted flaps and hydraulic tricycle landing gear of exceptional track but short length, placing the parked aircraft low on the ground. The introduction was delayed by numerous trivial modifications and even when service use began in 1957 pupils were first trained on the T-34. Altogether 534 T-37As were built, but all were brought up to the standard of the T-37B, of 1959, which had more powerful J69 engines, improved radio, navaids and revised instrument panel. After 41 had been converted to A-37As further T-37As were bought in 1957 to bring the total of this model to 447. They serve in roughly equal numbers with the advanced T-38A at all the USAF's pilot schools: 12th Flying Training Wing at Randolph; 14th at Columbus (Miss); 47th at Laughlin; 64th at Reese; 71st at Vance; 80th at Sheppard and 82nd at Williams.

The A-37 was derived to meet a need in the early 1960s for a light attack aircraft to fly Co-In (counter-insurgent) missions. Cessna had previously produced two T-37C armed trainers (many of this model were later supplied to Foreign Aid recipients, including South Vietnam in the 1960s),

and later these aircraft were then rebuilt as AT-37 prototypes (designation YAT-37D) with much more powerful engines and airframes restressed for increased weights which, in stages, were raised to 14,000lb (6,350kg). No fewer than eight underwing pylons plus wingtip tanks were added, giving a great weapon-carrying capability whilst offering performance significantly higher than that of the trainer. Redesignated A-37A, a squadron converted from T-37Bs on the production line was evaluated in Vietnam in 1967. Altogether 39 A-37As were built by converting T-37Bs on the line, followed by 511 of the regular USAF production model with full-rated J85 engines, 6g structure, flight-refuelling probe, greater internal tankage and other changes. The A-37 Dragonfly proved valuable in south-east Asia, where many were left in South Vietnamese hands after the US withdrawal. After the end of the US involvement the A-37B was withdrawn from regular USAF service but it continues to equip a Reserve wing and two Air National Guard groups. The AFR's 434th TFW flies the A-37B at Grissom AFB, Bunker Hill, Indiana, and the ANG units are the 174th TFG (Syracuse, NY) and the 175th (Baltimore, Md).

Below: Quite apart from the impressive array of tanks and bombs the A-37B Dragonfly bristles with communications and other mission avionic aerials not present on the T-37A trainer.

de Havilland Canada C-7

DHC-4 C-7A, C-7B

Origin: The de Havilland Aircraft of Canada, Toronto.
Type: STOL tactical transport.
Engines: Two 1,450hp Pratt & Whitney R-2000-7M2 Twin Wasp 14-cylinder.
Weights: Empty (A) 16,795lb (7,618kg), (B) 18,260lb (8,283kg); loaded (A) 26,000lb (11,794kg), (B) 31,300lb (14,198kg).
Performance: Maximum speed 216mph 9348km/h); typical cruising speed, 182mph (293km/h); initial climb 1,355ft (413m)/min; service ceiling, (A) 27,700ft (8,443m), (B) 24,800ft (7,559m); range (B) from 242 miles (389km) with max payload of 8,40lb (3,964kg) to 1,307 miles (2,103km) with maximum fuel; takeoff or landing over 50ft (15m), about 1,200ft (366m).
Armament: None.
History: First flight 30 July 1958; service delivery (US Army inventory) January 1961.

Fairchild C-123 Provider

C-123K

Origin: Fairchild Engine and Airplane Corporation, Hagerstown, Md (now Fairchild Republic Company, Farmingdale, NY).
Type: Tactical airlift transport.
Engines: Two 2,500hp Pratt & Whitney R-2800-99W Double Wasp 18-cylinder plus two 2,850lb (1,293kg) thrust GE J85-17 auxiliary turbojets.
Dimensions: Span 110ft 0in (33.53m); length 76ft 3in (23.92m); wing area 1,223sq ft (113.6m²).
Weights: Empty 35,366lb (16,042kg); loaded 60,000lb (27,216kg).
Performance: Maximum speed (with jets) 228mph (367km/h); maximum cruising speed, 173mph (278km/h); initial climb (no jets) 1,150ft (351m)/min; service ceiling 29,000ft (8,839m); range with maximum payload of 15,000lb (6,804kg), 1,035 miles (1,666km).
Armament: None.
History: First flight (XC-123) 14 October 1949, (K) 27 May 1966.

Development: The history of this tactical transport goes back to Chase Aircraft, of Trenton, NJ. Here the largest of a series of advanced stressed-skin transports and gliders (including a four-jet transport) was designed by M. Stoukoff in 1949, won an Air Force order for 300 but fell down when Kaiser-Frazer failed to build them. Fairchild stepped in, bought Chase and delivered the 300 on schedule. So good were these machines that they were updated in many ways, the final C-123K model having underwing-jet pods. Typical loads include trucks, artillery, 61 troops or 50 litter (stretcher) patients with six sitting wounded and six attendants. The C-123K still equips two AFRES units, the 302nd TAW at Rickenbacker AFB, Ohio, and the 439th (with C-130s) at Westover AFB, Mass.

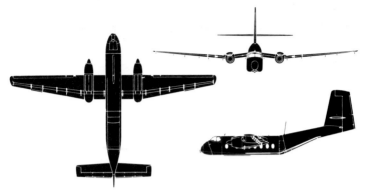

Above: Three-view of C-7A Caribou (without radar).

Development: A specialized STOL (short takeoff and landing) transport aimed mainly at the military market, the piston-engined Caribou has a fairly small interior roughly with the capacity and load capability of a C-47 (DC-3) but with a full-section rear loading ramp which can also be used for air dropping. Features include high-lift flaps, manual controls from a dual cockpit, nose radar and pneumatic boot deicers on all leading edges. The US Army purchased 159 of which the final 103 were to a later standard with increased weight. Normal loads included 32 troops or two Jeeps or similar small vehicles. In 1967, at the height of their involvement in Vietnam, a political decision transferred these aircraft to the Air Force. They still equip the ANG's 135th TAG, at Baltimore, assigned to MAC.

Left: A radar-equipped C-7A serving with the AF Reserves.

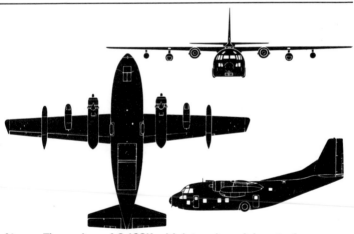

Above: Three-view of C-123K with jet pods and drop tanks.

Below: A recent picture of a C-123K, AF No 64-669.

51

Fairchild A-10 Thunderbolt II

A-10A, A-10/T, A-10/NAW

Origin: Fairchild Republic Company, Farmingdale, NY.

Type: Close-support attack aircraft.

Engines: Two 9,065lb (4,112kg) thrust General Electric TF34-100 turbofans.

Dimensions: Span 57ft 6in (17.53m); length 53ft 4in (16.26m); height (regular) 14ft 8in (4.47m), (NAW) 15ft 4in (4.67m); wing area 506sq ft (47m²).

Weights: Empty 21,519lb (9761kg); forward airstrip weight (no fuel but four Mk 82 bombs and 750 rounds) 32,730lb (14,846kg); maximum 50,000lb (22,680kg). Operating weight empty, 24,918lb (11,302kg), (NAW) 28,630lb (12,986kg).

Performance: Maximum speed, (max weight, A-10A) 423mph (681km/h), (NAW) 420mph (676km/h); cruising speed at sea level (both) 345mph (555km/h); stabilized speed below 8,000ft (2,440m) in 45° dive at weight 35,125lb (15,932kg), 299mph (481km/h); maximum climb at basic design weight of 31,790lb (14,420kg), 6,000ft (1,828m)/min; service ceiling, not stated; takeoff run to 50ft (15m) at maximum weight, 4,000ft (1,220m); operating radius in CAS mission with 1.8 hour loiter and reserves, 288 miles (463km); radius for single deep strike penetration, 620 miles (1,000km); ferry range with allowances, 2,542 miles (4091km).

Armament: One GAU-8/A Avenger 30mm seven-barrel gun with 1,174 rounds, total external ordnance load of 16,000lb (7,257kg) hung on 11 pylons, three side-by-side on body and four under each wing; several hundred combinations of stores up to individual weight of 5,000lb (2,268kg) with maximum total weight 14,638lb (6,640kg) with full internal fuel.

History: First flight (YA-10A) 10 May 1972; (production A-10A) 21 October 1975, (NAW) 4 May 1979. ▶

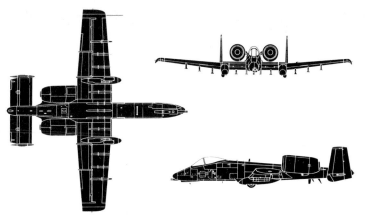

Above: Three-view of standard A-10A without Pave Penny pod.

Below left: Condensation vapour shimmers above the wings and streams from the downturned tips as an A-10A of the 354th TFW pulls round in a tight turn above the forests of South Carolina. The white missiles under the wing are AGM-65A Maverick precision guidance weapons (normally six carried).

Below: An unusual shot of an A-10A peeling off taken from the right-hand seat of an A-37B. Clean manoeuvrability is good.

Bottom: With a straight-wing aircraft as big as a small airliner, and very much slower, it might be thought A-10 pilots felt second-class citizens. These noses quash such an idea stone dead!

▶**Development:** After prolonged study of lightweight Co-In and light armed reconnaissance aircraft the Air Force in 1967 initiated the A-X programme for a new-generation CAS (close air support) aircraft. It had never had such an aircraft, this mission being previously flown by fighters, bombers, attack and even FAC platforms, including such diverse types as the F-105 and A-1. Emphasis in A-X was not on speed but on lethality against surface targets (especially armour), survivability against ground fire (not including SAMs), heavy ordnance load and long mission endurance. Low priority was paid to advanced nav/attack avionics, the fit being officially described as 'austere'. After a major competition the Northrop A-9A and Fairchild A-10A were pitted against each other in a flyoff contest throughout 1972, after which the A-10A was announced the Air Force's choice on 18 January 1973. Including six DT&E (development, test and evaluation) aircraft the planned force was to number 733, to be deployed in TAC wings in the USA and Europe, and also to a growing number of AFR and ANG squadrons.

Right: Seen over the desert in 1981, the N/AW (Night/Adverse Weather) A-10A is a company-sponsored two-seater with radar in the left gear pod, FLIR in the right and external laser and TV.

The original A-10A was a basically simple single-seater, larger than most tactical attack aircraft and carefully designed as a compromise between capability, survivability and low cost. As an example of the latter many of the major parts, including flaps, main landing gears and movable tail surfaces, are interchangeable left/right, and systems and engineering features were designed with duplication and redundancy to survive parts being shot away. The unusual engine location minimizes infra-red signature and makes it almost simple to fly with one engine inoperative or even shot off. Weapon pylons were added from tip to tip, but the chief tank-killing ordnance is the gun, the most powerful (in terms of muzzle horsepower) ever mounted in an aircraft, firing milk-bottle-size rounds at rates hydraulically controlled at 2,100 or 4,200 shots/min. The gun is mounted 2° nose-down and offset to the left so that the firing barrel is always on the centrelilne (the nose landing gear being offset to the right).

The basic aircraft has a HUD (head-up display), good communications fit ▶

Left: An A-10A demonstrates its agility in a pull-up at very low level over a column of USA M60 battle tanks. The long store under the right wing is a Westinghouse ALQ-119 ECM pod.

Below: Taken during early evaluation trials with one of the YA-10A prototypes, this photograph shows ammunition being made up into belts. This aircraft has only a small gun of 20mm size.

and both Tacan and an inertial system, as well as ECM and radar homing and warning. Deliveries to the 354th TFW at Myrtle Beach, South Carolina, began in 1977, and over 500 have since been received by units in TAC, USAFE (including the 81st TFW in England and 601 TCW at Sembach) and various other commands including the Reserve and ANG. Though relatively slow and ungainly the 'Thud-II' has won over any pilot who might have looked askance at it, and has demonstrated in its first 100,000 hours the ability to do a major job under increasingly hazardous conditions and at the lowest height normally practised by any jet aircraft. Nevertheless attrition at 9 aircraft per 100,000 hours in 1981 was double expectation, resulting in an

Below: A beautiful portrait at dusk of a Maverick-armed A-10A of the 354th TFW. There seems no doubt that, in the long term, this model will be updated for all-weather use with more sensors.

increase in the overall programme to 825 to sustain the desired force to the mid-1990s. Significantly, half the 60 aircraft in the FY81 budget were two-seaters, which though priced $600,000 higher are expected to effect savings by reducing the demand for chase aircraft.

In 1979 Fairchild flew a company-funded NAW (night/adverse weather) demonstrator with augmented avionics and a rear cockpit for a WSO seated at a higher level and with good forward view. Both the regular and NAW aircraft can carry a Pave Penny laser seeker pod under the nose, vital for laser-guilded munitions, and the NAW also has a Ferranti laser ranger, FLIR (forward-looking infra-red), GE low-light TV and many other items including a Westinghouse multimode radar with WSO display. It is probable that during the rest of the decade A-10As will be brought at least close to the NAW standard, while the two-seat NAW might be procured alongside or in place of future buys of the basic A-10A.

General Dynamics F-16 Fighting Falcon

F-16A, B

Origin: General Dynamics Corporation, Fort Worth, Texas.

Type: Multi-role righter (B) operational fighter/trainer.

Engine: One 23,840lb (10,814kg) thrust Pratt & Whitney F100-200 afterburning turbofan.

Dimensions: Span 31ft 0in (9.449m) 32ft 10in/1.01m over missile fins); length (both versions, excl probe) 47ft 7.7in (14.52m); wing area 300.0 sq ft (27.87m²).

Weights: Empty (A) 15,137lb (6,866kg), (B) 15,778lb (7,157kg); loaded (AAMs only) (A) 23,357lb (10,594kg), (B) 22,814lb (10,348kg), (max external load) (both) 35,400lb (16,057kg). (Block 25 on) 37,500lb (17,010kg).

Performance: Maximum speed (both, AAMs only) 1,350mph (2,173km/h, Mach 2.05) at 40,000ft (12.19km); maximum at SL, 915mph (1,472km/h, Mach 1.2); initial climb (AAMs only) 50,000ft (15.24km)/min; service ceiling, over 50,000ft (15.24km); tactical radius (A, six Mk 82, internal fuel, HI-LO-HI) 340 miles (547km); ferry range, 2,415 miles (3,890km).

Armament: One M61A-1 20mm gun with 500/515 rounds, centreline pylon for 300 US gal (m1,136lit) drop tank or 2,200lb (998kg) bonb, inboard wing plyons for 3,500lb (1,587kg) each, middle wing pylons for 2,500lb (1,134kg) each (being uprated under MSIP-1 to 3,500lb), outer wing pylons for 250lb (113.4kg), all ratings being at 9 g.

History: First flight (YF) 20 January 1974, (production F-16A) 7 August 1978; service delivery (A) 17 August 1978.

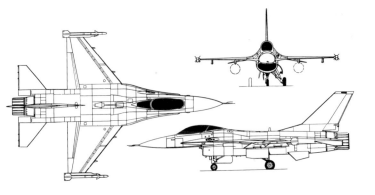

Above: Three-view of standard F-16A-GD-15.

Development: The Fighting Falcon originated through a belief by the Air Force that there might be a more cost/effective fighter than the outstanding but necessarily expensive F-15. In a Lightweight Fighter (LWF) programme of 1972 it sought bids from many design teams, picked GD's Model 401 and ▶

Left: An F-16B two-seater of the 388th TFW, Hill AFB. The AAMs are AIM-9J1 Sidewinders.

Below: An F-16A of the 388th in low-visibility markings, seen in late 1979 at Nellis AFB with an AN/ASQ data-link probe on one wing and AIM-9L on the other.

59

▶Northrop's simplified P.530 and evaluated two prototypes of each as the YF-16 and YF-17. GD's engineering team created a totally new aircraft with such advanced features as relaxed static stability (a basic distribution of shapes and masses to attain greater combat agility, overcoming a marginal longitudinal stability by the digital flight-control system), large wing/body flare to enhance lift at high angles of attack and house a gun and extra fuel, a straight wing with hinged leading and trailing flaps used to increase manoeuvrability in combat (the trailing surfaces being rapid-action flaperons), fly-by-wire electrically signalled flight controls, a futuristic cockpit with reclining zero/zero seat for best resistance to g, with a sidestick controller instead of a control column and one-piece canopy/windscreen of blown polycarbonate, and a miniature multi-mode pulse-doppler radar. On 13 January 1975 the Air Force announced full development of the F-16 not just as a simple day air-combat fighter but also to meet a greatly expanded requirement calling for comprehensive all-weather navigation and weapon delivery in the air/surface role.

This vitally important programme growth was triggered largely by the recognition that there existed a near-term European market, and in June

Above: An F-16A of the 388th burdened by two AIM-9L, two AIM-9J, two Mk 84 (2,000-lb, 907-kg) bombs, two 370-US gal (1700-litre) drop tanks and a Westinghouse AN/ALQ-119 (V) ECM pod.

A pair of Fighting Falcons from Hill AFB. Later a suitable grey paint was discovered for the radome, reducing visibility.

1975 orders were announced by four European NATO countries (Belgium, Denmark, Netherlands and Norway). These organized with GD and P&WA a large multinational manufacturing programme which in the longer term has greatly expanded the production base. In July 1975 the Air Force ordered six pre-production F-16As and two F-16Bs with tandem dual controls and internal fuel reduced from 1,072.5 US gal (4,060lit) to 889.8 (3,368). Both introduced a flight-refuelling boom receptacle (into which a probe can be inserted) and provision for a 300 US gal (1,136lit) centreline drop tank and two 370gal (1,400lit) wing tanks. All eight aircraft were delivered by June 1978, by which time the Air Force had announced a programme for 1,184 F-16As and 204-F-16Bs, with the name Fighting Falcon.

Few aircraft have been as excitedly received as the F-16, which by sheer engineering excellence and painstaking development is as close to the optimum combat aircraft as it is possible to get in its timescale. Even so, it was naturally prey to occasional troubles, notably the prolonged stall-stagnation engine difficulty that had earlier hit the F-15 with an almost identical engine. Following intensive test programmes at Edwards, Nellis and by an MOT&E (multi-national operational test and evaluation) team the ▶

Above: In sharp contrast, this F-16A is flying in the minimum air-combat configuration, with no stores other than a pair of AIM-9J on the tip rails. Thrust/weight ratio can exceed unity.

▶388th TFW at Hill AFB, Utah, began to convert on 6 January 1979 and has subsequently not only achieved a string of 'firsts' with the F-16 but has set impressive records in the process. Next came the 56th TFW at MacDill, Florida, followed by the 474th at Nellis, Nevada, the 8th TFW at Kunsan, S Korea, the 50th TFW at Hahn, W. Germany (in USAFE) and the 363rd at Shaw, S. Carolina. Thanks to the large production base and wide international deployment (extending to Israel, S Korea, Egypt, Pakistan and other countries beyond those previously listed) global deployment of Air Force F-16 units is proving exceptionally simple, the aircraft having swiftly attained an exceptional level of reliabilty which is enhanced by outstanding maintenance and self-test features.

Enthusiasm by pilots and ground crew has been exceptional, but an event which dramatically highlighted how far the F-16 had come since 1974 was its first participation in a numerically scored inter-service competition. In the searching USAF/RAF contest held at RAF Lossiemouth on 16-19 June 1981 teams of F-16s (388th TFW), F-111s, Jaguars and Buccaneers were required under realistic wartime scenarios to penetrate defended airspace, engage hostile fighters and bomb airfields and road convoys. The F-16s were the only aircraft to hit all assigned surface targets, while in air combat their score was 86 kills against no losses; rival teams suffered 42 losses and ▶

Above: Low-visibility F-16A with instrumentation transmitter on right wing and ALQ-119 jammer pod on centreline.

Below: Shallow dive attack with two Mk 84 bombs by F-16A also carrying two tanks, two AIM-9L, two AIM-9J and jammer pod.

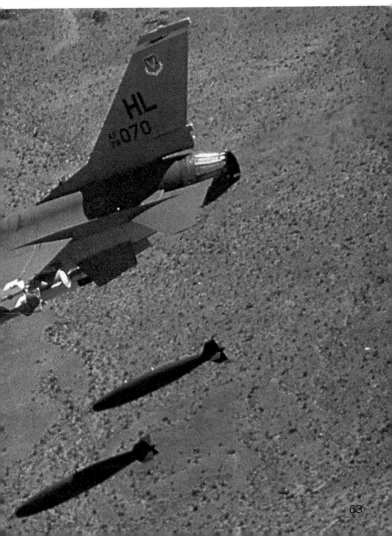

▶collectively scored but a single kill. The F-16 also scored very much better against Rapier SAM threats, while in the ground-crew part of the contest the 388th achieved an average turnround time between sorties of 10½ minutes, including refuelling, loading six Mk 82 bombs and 515 rounds of ammunition. Since its introduction to TAC the F-16 has had the highest Mission Capable Rate in the command, and has been the only multirole aircraft to achieve the command goal of 70%.

In 1982 production had passed 600 aircraft, with plenty of spare capacity at Fort Worth for up to 45 per month if necessary. Though this excellent output was attained by sticking to an agreed standard of build, improvements

Below: A F-16A of the 388th TFW, in the low-visibility markings now standard in Tactical Air Command. Tail designator letters for the next two wings to be completely equipped with the F-16 were: NA, 474th TFW, Nellis AFB; MC, 56th TFW, MacDill.

have been continual, and many more are in prospect. During production the inlet was strengthened to carry EO/FLIR and laser pods, a graphite/epoxy tailplane of larger size was introduced to match increased gross weight (see data), and the central computer and avionics were changed for a much 'expanded package'. Later the 30mm GEpod gun, Maverick missile, Lantirn and AMRAAM advanced missile will be introduced, the new AAM being linked with the programmable APG-66 radar for stand-off interception capability. Later still the striking bat-like SCAMP (supersonic-cruise aircraft modification program) may result in still higher performance with double bombloads.

Below: The F-16B being used to develop an F-16 with Wild Weasel anti-radar capability. The weapons installed here are AIM-9J (tips), AGM-45 Shrike (stations 2 and 8) and AGM-88 HARM (High-speed Anti-Radiation Missile) (stations 2 and 7).

General Dynamics F-106 Delta Dart

F-106A, B

Origin: General Dynamics Convair Division, San Diego, California.
Type: All-weather interceptor, (B) operational trainer.
Engine: One 24,500lb (11,130kg) thrust Pratt & Whitney J75-17 afterburning turbojet.
Dimensions: Span 38ft 3in (11.67m); length (both) 70ft 8¾in (21.55m); wing area 661.5 sq ft (61.52m²).
Weights: Empty (A) about 24,420lb (11,077kg); loaded (normal) 34,510lb (15,668kg).
Performance: Maximum speed (both) 1,525mph (2,455km/h) or Mach 2.3 at 36,000ft (11km); initial climb, about 29,000ft (8,839m)/min; service ceiling 57,000ft (17,374m); range with drop tanks 1,800 miles (2,897km).
Armament: One 20mm M61A-1 gun, two AIM-4F plus two AIM-4G Falcons, plus one AIR-2A or -2G Genie nuclear rocket.
History: First flight (aerodynamic prototype) 26 December 1956, (B) 9 April 1958; squadron delivery June 1959.

Development: Derived from the earlier F-102 Delta Dagger, the F-106 had a maximum speed approximately twice as high and completely met the requirements of Aerospace Defense Command (Adcom) for a manned interceptor to defend the continental United States. Linked via its complex and bulky MA-1 electronic fire-control system through a digital data link into the nationwide SAGE (semi-automatic ground environment), the 106 served much longer than intended and in fact never did see a successor, despite the continued threat of the manned bomber, though there were numerous engineering improvements and some substantial updates including the addition of the gun (in a neat installation in the missile bay, causing a

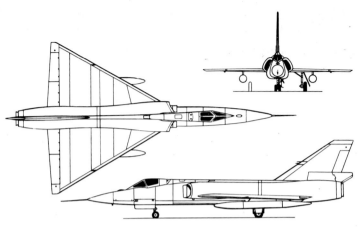

Above: Three-view of F-106A with IR seeker ahead of windscreen.

slight ventral bulge) as well as improved avionics, an infra-red sensor of great sensitivity facing ahead for detecting heat from hostile aircraft and assisting the lock-on of AAMs, and a flight-refuelling boom receptacle. Convair completed many other studies including improved electric power system, solid-state computer, the AIMS (aircraft identification monitoring system) and an enhanced-capability variant for Awacs control. The last of 277 F-106As and 63 tandem-seat F-106B armed trainers were delivered in 1961. Adcom was disbanded in 1980 and the F-106 is now flown only by fighter interceptor units in TAC and in the ANG, assigned to TAC.

Below: Darts of one of the last surviving FISs, now part of Tactical Air Command. A replacement is being discussed.

General Dynamics F-111

F-111A, D, E and F, FB-111A and EF-111A

Origin: (except EF) General Dynamics Corporation, Fort Worth, Texas; (EF) Grumman Aerospace Corporation, Bethpage, NY.

Type: A,D,E,F, all-weather attack; FB, strategic attack; EF, tactical ECM jammer.

Powerplant: Two Pratt & Whitney TF30 afterburning turbofans, as follow, (A, C, EF) 18,500lb (8,390kg) TF30-3, (D,E) 19,600lb (8,891kg) TF30-9, (FB) 20,350lb (9,231kg) TF30-7, (F) 25,100lb (11,385kg) TF30-100.

Dimensions: Span (fully spread) (A,D,E,F,EF) 63ft 0in (19.2m), (FB) 70ft 0in (21.34m), (fully swept) (A,D,E,F,E,F) 31ft 11½in (9.74m), (FB) 33ft 11in (10.34m); length (except EF) 73ft 6in (22.4m), (EF) 77ft 1.6in (23.51m); wing area (A,D,E,F,EF, gross, 16°) 525 sq ft (48.77m²)

Weights: Empty (A) 46,172lb (20,943kg), (D) 49,090lb (22,267kg), (E) about 47,000lb (21,319kg), (EF) 53,418lb) (24,230kg), (F) 47,481lb (21,537kg), (FB) close to 50,000lb (22,680kg); loaded (A) 91,500lb (41,500kg), (D,E) 92,500lb (41,954kg), (F) 100,000lb (45,360kg), (FB) 114,300lb (51,846kg), (EF) 87,478lb (39,680kg).

Performance: Maximum speed at 36,000ft (11km), clean and with max afterburner, (A,D,E) Mach 2.2, 1,450mph (2,335km/h), (FB) Mach 2, 1,320mph (2,124km/h), (F) Mach 2.5, 1,653mph (2,660km/h), (EF) Mach 1.75, 1,160mph (1,865km/h); cruising speed, penetration, 571mph (919km/h); initial climb (EF) 3,592ft (1,95m)/min; service ceiling at combat weight, max afterburner, (A) 51,000ft (15,500m), (F) 60,000ft (18,290m), (EF) 54,700ft (16,670m); range with max internal fuel (A,D) 3,165 miles (5,093km), (F) 2,925 miles (4,707km), (EF) 2,484 miles (3,998km); takeoff run (A) 4,000ft (1,219m), (F) under 3,000ft (914m), (FB) 4,700ft (1,433m), (EF) 3,250ft (991m).

Armament: Internal weapon bay for two B43 bombs or (D,F) one B43 and one M61 gun; three pylons under each wing (four inboard swivelling with wing, outers being fixed and usable only at 16°, otherwise being jettisoned) for max external load 31,500lb (14,288kg); (FB only) provision for up to six SRAM, two internal; (EF) no armament.

History: First flight 21 December 1964, service delivery (A) June 1967 (EF) July 1981.

▶

Below: An F-111A of the 366th TFW (Mountain Home AFB, Idaho) lets go 24 bombs during a max-conventional load attack mission.

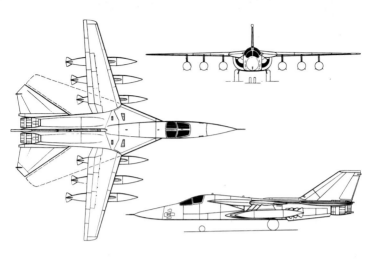

Above: Three-view of A,D,E or F model (gun not fitted).

Above: An early F-111E on test with a white radome; this model has since 1970 been deployed in England (20th TFW).

Below: View of an F-111 of TAC as it edges in under a KC-135 with its boom receptacle door open above the fuselage.

▶**Development:** In 1960 the Department of Defense masterminded the TFX (tactical fighter experimental) as a gigantic programme to meet all the fighter and attack needs of the Air Force, Navy and Marine Corps, despite the disparate requirements of these services, and expected the resultant aircraft to be bought throughout the non-Communist world. In fact, so severe were the demands for weapon load and, in particular, mission range that on the low power available the aircraft had inadequate air-combat capability and in fact it was destined never to serve in this role, though it is still loosely described as a 'tactical fighter'. After prolonged technical problems involving escalation in weight, severe aerodynamic drag, engine/inlet mismatch and, extending into the early 1970s, structural failures, the F-111 eventually matured as the world's best long-range interdiction attack aircraft which in the hands of dedicated and courageous Air Force crews pioneered the new art of 'skiing'—riding the ski-toe locus of a TFR (terrain-following radar) over hills, mountains and steep-sided valleys in blind conditions, in blizzards or by night, holding a steady 200ft (91m) distance from the ground at high-subsonic speed, finally to plant a bomb automatically within a few metres of a previously computed target.

Basic features of the F-111 include a variable-sweep 'swing wing' (the first in production in the world) with limits of 16° and 72.5°, with exceptional high-lift devices, side-by-side seating for the pilot and right-seat navigator (usually also a pilot) or (EF) electronic-warfare officer, large main gears with low-pressure tyres for no-flare landings on soft strips (these prevent the carriage of ordnance on fuselage pylons), a small internal weapon bay, very great internal fuel capacity (typically 5,022 US gal, 19,010 litres), and emergency escape by jettisoning the entire crew compartment, which has its own parachutes and can serve as a survival shelter or boat.

General Dynamics cleared the original aircraft for service in 2½ years, and ▶

Above: By far the best of the tactical attack models, the F-111F equips the 48th TFW at RAF Lakenheath, England. The avionics represent an attempt to combine some of the advanced features of the Mk II system (F-111D) without the latter's frustrating costs and problems, while the engine is much more powerful than that of any other F-111 (and much more powerful than any TF30 fitted to the Navy's Grumman F-14 Tomcat for that matter!).

Below: A pair of FB-111A bombers from Strategic Air Command are seen here in long-range cruise with no external load except a pair of 500-US gal (2271-litre) tanks. Two Mk 43, Mk 57 or TX-61 bombs may be aboard.

▶built 141 of this F-111A version, which equips 366TFW at Mountain Home AFB, Idaho (others have been reserved for conversion into the EF-111A). It is planned to update the A by fitting a digital computer to the original analog-type AJQ-20A nav/bomb system, together with the Air Force standard INS and a new control/display set. The F-111E was similar but had larger inlet ducts and engines of slightly greater power; 94 were delivered and survivors equip the 20th TFW at Upper Heyford, England. These are to receive the same updates as the A. Next came the F-111D, which at great cost was fitted with an almost completely different avionic system of a basically digital nature including the APQ-30 attack radar, APN-189 doppler and HUDs for both crew-members. This aircraft had great potential but caused severe technical and manpower problems in service and never fully realized its capabilities, though it remains a major advance on the A and E. The 96 built have always equipped the 27th TFW at Cannon AFB, New Mexico. The F-111F is by far the best of all tactical F-111 versions, almost entirely because Pratt & Whitney at last produced a really powerful TF30 which incorporated many other advanced features giving enhanced life with fewer problems. With much greater performance than any other model the F could if necessary double in an air-combat role though it has no weapons for this role except the gun and if necessary AIM-9. The 106 of this model served at Mountain Home until transfer to the 48th TFW in England, at Lakenheath. The most important of all F-111 post-delivery modifications has been the conversion of the F force to use the Pave Tack pod, normally stowed in the weapon bay but rotated out on a cradle for use. This complex package provides a day/night all-weather capability to acquire, track, designate and hit surface targets using EO, IR or laser guided weapons. The first squadron to convert was the 48th TFW's 494th TFS, in September 1981. Their operations officer, Maj Bob Rudiger, has said: 'Important targets that once required several aircraft can now be disabled with a single Pave Tack aircraft, the radar tells the pod where to look, and the laser allows us to put the weapon precisely on target.'

The long-span FB-111A was bought to replace the B-58 and early models of B-52 in SAC, though the raising price resulted in a cut in procurement from 210 to 76, lentering service in October 1969. It has so-called Mk IIB avionics, derived from those of the D but configured for SAC missions using nuclear bombs or SRAMs. With strengthened structure and landing gear the FB has a capability of carrying 41,250lb (18,711kg) of bombs, made up of 50 bombs of 825lb (nominal 750lb size) each. This is not normally used, and the outer pylons associated with this load are not normally installed. The FB equips SAC's 380th BW at Plattsburgh AFB, NY, and the 509th at Pease, New Hampshire. No go-ahead has been received for numerous extremely capable stretched FB versions.

Left: F-111F No 70-369 cruises above fine-weather cumulus clouds as it heads across England for practice TFR (terrain-following radar) flight and a simulated bomb drop on an instrumented range in the Isle of Man.

Below: This EF-111A still bears its original tail number 66-051, showing it was one of the fourth block of the F-111A version before its total reconstruction. The Air Force has a desperate need for considerably more advanced EW (electronic-warfare) platforms than the 42 of this type which it hopes to be able to afford.

Above: The first production EF-111A was former F-111A No 66-049, seen here on flight test at Grumman's facility at Calverton, NY.

Last of the F-111 variants, the EF-111A is the USAF's dedicated EW platform, managed by Grumman (partner on the original Navy F-111B version) and produced by rebuilding F-111As. The USA acknowledges the Soviet Union to have a lead in both ground and air EW, and thousands of radars and other defence emitters in Eastern Europe would make penetration by NATO aircraft extremely dangerous. The vast masking power of the EF-110A, which equals that of the Navy EA-6B and in fact uses almost the same ALQ-99E tac-jam system (but with a crew of only two instead of four), is expected to be able to suppress these 'eyes' and enable NATO aircraft to survive. An aerodynamic prototype flew in March 1977, the ALQ-99 was flying in an F-111 in May 1977, and production deliveries began in mid-1981 to the 366th TFW. The Air Force plans to have 42 aircraft rebuilt as EFs, for service with all USAFE penetrating attack units and others in TAC and possibly other commands.

Lockheed C-5A Galaxy

C-5A

Origin: Lockheed-Georgia Company, Marietta, Ga.
Type: Heavy strategic airlift transport.
Powerplant: Four 41,000lb (18,597kg) thrust General Electric TF39-1 turbofans.
Dimensions: Span 222ft 8½in (67.88m); length 247ft 10in (75.54m); height 65ft 1½in (19.85m); wing area 6,200sq ft (576.0m²).
Weights: Empty (basic operating) 337,937lb (153,285kg), loaded (2,25g) 769,000lb (348,810kg).
Performance: Maximum speed (max weight, 25,000ft/7,620m) 571mph (760km/h); normal long-range cruising speed, 518mph (834km/h); initial climb at max wt., rated thrust, 1,800ft (549m)/min; service ceiling, (615,000lb/278,950kg) 34,000ft (10.36km); range with design payload of 220, 967lb (100,228kg), 3,749 miles (6,033km); range with 112,600lb (51,074kg) payload, 6,529 miles 7,991 miles (12,860km); takeoff distance at max wt. over 50ft (15m), 8,400ft (2,560m); landing from 50ft (15m), 3,600ft (1,097m).
Armament: None.
History: First flight 30 June 1968; service delivery, 17 December 1969; final delivery from new, May 1973.

Development: Growing appreciation of the need for an extremely large logistics transport to permit deployment of the heaviest hardware items on a global basis led in 1963 to the CX-HLS (Heavy Logistics System) specification calling for a payload of 250,000lb (113,400kg) over a coast-to-coast range and half this load over the extremely challenging unrefuelled range of 8,000 miles (12,875km); it also demanded the abililty to fly such loads into a 4,000ft (1,220m) rough forward airstrip. Such performance was theoretically possible using a new species of turbofan, of high bypass ratio, much more powerful than existing engines. In August 1965 GE won the engine contract, and two months later Lockheed won the C-5A aircraft. Design was undertaken under extreme pressure, the wing being assigned to CDI, a group of British engineers from the cancelled HS.115 and TSR.2 programmes. About half the value of each airframe was subcontracted to ▶

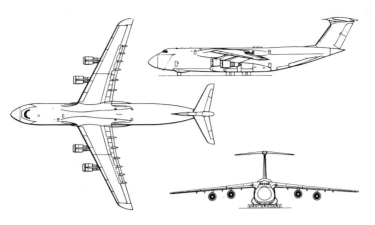

Above: Three-view of C-5A Galaxy as delivered to MAC.

Above: First takeoff by the prototype on 30 June 1968; subsequently the TF39 engine was made almost free from visible smoke.

Above: An almost grotesque appearance results from a camera resting on the ground and the nose door partly open.

Left: Production took place in batches of 53 and 23 (plus five prototypes). This is 68-0216 from the main block of 53.

▶suppliers in the US and Canada, and construction of the first aircraft (66-8303) began as early as August 1966.

Meeting the requirements proved impossible, and cost-inflation reduced the total buy from 115 (six squadrons) to 81 (four squadrons), of which 30 were delivered by the end of 1970. As a cargo airlifter the C-5A proved in a class of its own, with main-deck width of 19ft (5.79m) and full-section access at front and rear. The upper deck houses the flight crew of five, a rest area for a further 15 and a rear (aft of the wing) area with 75 seats. Features include high-lift slats and flaps, an air-refuelling receptacle, advanced forward-looking radars and a unique landing gear with 28 wheels offering the required 'high flotation' for unpaved surfaces, as weel as free castoring to facilitate ground manoeuvring, an offset (20° to left or right) swivelling capability for use in crosswinds, fully modulating anti-skid brakes and the ability to kneel to bring the main deck close to the ground. Despite highly publicized faults, most of which were quickly rectified, the C-5A was soon

Above: C-5A No 67-0171 in a remarkably tight turn at low level.

Below: The C-5A (this is 69-0013) dwarfs even the KC-10A.

giving invaluable service; but a deep-rooted difficulty was that the wing accrued fatigue damage much more rapidly than had been predicted. Several costly modification programmes proved incomplete solutions, and in 1978 Lockheed's proposal for the introduction of a new wing was accepted. This wing uses a totally different detailed design in different materials, and though the moving surfaces are largely unchanged even these are to be manufactured again, the slats, ailerons and flap tracks for the second time being assigned to Canadair. Between 1982-87 all 77 surviving aircraft are to be re-winged. This is being done with minimal reduction in airlift capability by MAC's 60th MAW at Travis, 436th at Dover, Delaware, and 443rd at Altus AFB, Oklahoma.

In 1982 the Reagan administration recommended purchase of an additional 50 aircraft costing $8 billion, instead of C-17s. These C-5Ns will have long crack-free airframe life, improved avionics and easier serviceability, but no engine details had been released in April 1982.

Above: Taken during manoeuvres with the USA in the United States this landing picture shows both the multi-segment flaps and the 28 landing wheels needed to confer 'flotation' for soft fields.

Lockheed C-130 Hercules

C-130A to P, DC-130, EC-130, HC-130, JHC-130, JC-130, MC-130, RC-130, WC-130.

Origin: Lockheed-Georgia Company, Marietta, Ga.

Type: Originally, multirole airlift transport; special variants, see text.

Powerplant: Four Allison T56 turboprops, (B and E families) 4,050ehp T56-7, (H family) 4,910ehp T56-15 flat-rated at 4,508ehp.

Dimensions: Span 132ft 7in (40.41m); length (basic) 97ft 9in (29.79m), (HC-130H, arms spread) 106ft 4in (32.41m); wing area 1,745sq ft (162.12m²).

Weights: Empty (basic E, H) 72,892lb (33 063kg); operating weight (H) 75,832lb (34,397kg); loaded (E,H) 155,000lb (70,310kg), max overload 175,000lb (79,380kg).

Performance: Maximum speed at 175,000lb (E, H), also max cruising speed, 386mph (621km/h); economical cruise, 345mph (556km/h); initial SL climb (E) 1,830ft (558m)/min, (H) 1,900ft (579m)/min; service ceiling at 155,000lb, (E) 23,000ft (7,010m), (H) 26,500ft (8,075m); range (H with max payload of 2,487 miles (4,002km; ferry range with reserves (H), 4,606 miles (7,412km); takeoff to 50ft (15m) (H at 175,000lb), 5,160ft (1,573m); landing from 50ft (15m) (H at 100,000lb/45,360kg), 2,700ft (823m).

Armament: Normally none.

History: First flight (YC-130A) 23 August 1954, (production C-130A) 7 April 1955; service delivery December 1956.

Development: When the Berlin Airlift and Korean war highlighted the need for more capable military transport aircraft, several obvious features were waiting to be combined in one design. Among these were a high wing and unobstructed cargo compartment, a flat level floor at truck-bed height above ▶

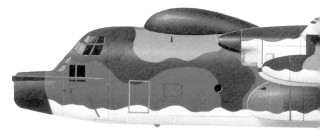

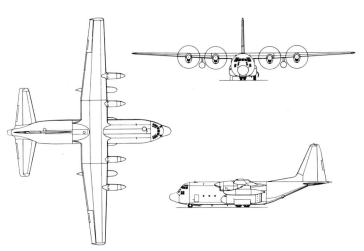

Above: Three-view of standard C-130E or C-130H.

Below: One of seven sub-variants equipped for the aerial recovery of spacecraft or other items or the pick-up of passengers from the ground. Main user is ARRS (Aerospace Rescue and Recovery Service) whose models included the HC-130H, JHC-130H, DC-130H, HC-130N and HC-130P.

Below: All models of C-130 (this is a standard C-130H) are cleared for unrestricted weight operation from unpaved airstrips.

Above: Fine picture of C-130H No 63-7798, in regular camouflage with one of the MAC airlift squadrons on inter-theatre duties.

▶ the ground, pressurization and air-conditioning, full-section rear door and vehicle ramp, turboprop propulsion for high performance, a modern flight deck with all-round vision, and retractable landing gear with 'high flotation' tyres for use from unprepared airstrips. All were incorporated in the Lockheed Model 82 which in June 1951 won an Air Force requirement for a new and versatile transport for TAC. By sheer good fortune the Allison single-shaft T56 turboprop matured at precisely the right time, along with a new species of advanced Aeroproducts or HamStan propeller and several other new-technology items including high-strength 2024 aluminium alloy, machined skin planks for the wings and cargo floor, metal/metal bonding and titanium alloys for the nacelles and flap skins. Another new feature was a miniature APU (auxiliary power unit) in one of the landing-gear blisters to provide ground power for air-conditioning and main-engine pneumatic starting.

Two YC-130 prototypes were built at Burbank, with 3,250hp T56-1 engines, but long before these were completed the programme was moved to the vast Government Plant 6 in Georgia which had been built to produce the B-29 under Bell management and restored to active use by Lockheed in January 1951. The new transport was ordered as the C-130A in September 1952 and the work phased in well with the tapering off of the B-47. When the 130, soon dubbed the Herky-bird, joined the 463rd Troop Carrier Wing at Ardmore in 1956 it caused a stir of a kind never before associated with a mere cargo transport. Pilots began to fly their big airlifters like fighters, and to explore the limits of what appeared to be an aircraft so willing it would do impossible demands. This was despite increases in permitted gross weight from 102,000lb to 116,000 and then to 124,200lb (56,335kg). At an early stage the nose grew a characteristic pimple from switching to the APN-59 radar, and provision was made for eight 1,000lb (454kg) Aerojet assisted takeoff rockets to be clipped to the sides of the fuselage, to augment the thrust of full-rated 3,750hp engines.

In December 1958 Lockheed flew the first extended-range C-130B with more powerful engines driving four-blade propellers. The Air Force bought 132 to supplement the 204 A-models, the latter progressively being rebuilt as AC-130 gunships, DC-130 drone (RPV) controllers, JC-130 spacecraft tracking and retrieval aircraft and C-130D wheel/ski aircraft with Arctic/Antarctic equipment. The next basic model, and bought in largest numbers (389), was the E, first flown on 25 August 1961. With this a minor ▶

Above: Delivery from high level of an armoured car by parachuted pallet; the aircraft is a MAC C-130H.

Below: Delivery of an M551 Sheridan light tank by the alternative method of ground-proximity extraction without parachutes.

Above: Exceptional C-130 force on manoeuvres at Dyess AFB, Texas.

▶structural rework enabled wing pylons to carry large drop tanks of 1,360 US gal (5,145lit), meeting the strategic range requirements of MATS (now MAC) and thus opening up a new market for the 130 beyond the tactical sphere. MATS (MAC) received 130 of the E model, and TAC re-equipped with 245 and transferred the A and B models to the ANG and Reserve, giving these reserve forces undreamed-of airlift capability. Some B-models were converted for other roles, new duties including weather reconnaissance (WC-130) and a single STOL aircraft with extra pod-mounted T56 engines supplying a boundary-layer control system, designated NC-130. Among currently serving rebuilds of the E are the EC-130E tactical command and control platform, with several unique avionic systems, and the MC-130E used with special avionics and low-level flight techniques for clandestine exfiltration and airdrop missions.

Latest basic type is the C-130H, first delivered in April 1975, with more powerful engines flat-rated at the previous level to give improved takeoff from hot/high airstrips. Variations include the HC-130H extended-range model for the Aerospace Rescue and Recovery Service with a fold-out nose installation for the snatching of people or payloads from the ground. The JHC-130H model has further gear for aerial recovery of space capsules. A more advanced model, with special direction-finding receivers but without long-range tanks, is the HC-130N. The HC-130P model combines the mid-air retrieval capability with a tanking and air-refuelling function for helicopters.

This evergreen aircraft is by far the most important Air Force tactical airlifter and fulfils a host of secondary functions. Though civil and RAF versions have been stretched to match capacity to payload, this has not been done by the USAF. Production continues, and six H models were ordered for the AFRes and ANG in July 1981. New roles being studied by the Air Force include the C-130H-MP maritime patroller with offshore surveillance equipment, and the CAML (cargo aircraft minelayer) system using hydraulically powered pallets for rapid-sequence deployment of large sea mines. Should CAML be adopted, Air Force C-130s could fly minelaying missions for the Navy.

Below: No longer in use, the AC-130A was the first AC-130 armed gunship version for truck-killing at night. Two 20-mm M61s are firing.

Top: A C-130—apparently an HC-130 of the ARRS—moving off during a 1979 exercise. Some models have heated ski landing gears.

Above: Though the gunship models are no longer active this advanced multi-sensor AC-130H was photographed in 1980.

Lockheed C-141 StarLifter

C-141A and B

Origin: Lockheed-Georgia Company, Marietta, Ga.

Type: Strategic airlift and aeromedical transport.

Powerplant: Four 21,000lb (9,525kg) thrust Pratt & Whitney TF33-7 turbofans.

Dimensions: Span 159ft 11in (48.74m); length (A) 145ft. 0in (44.2m), (B) 168ft 3½in (51.29m); wing area 3,228sq. ft (299.9m²).

Weights: Empty (A) 133,733lb (60,678kg), (B) 148,120lb (67,186kg); loaded (A) 316,600lb (143,600kg), (B) 343,000lb (155,585kg).

Performance: Maximum speed (A) 571mph (919km/h), (B, also max cruising speed) 566mph (910km/h); long-range cruising speed (both) 495mph (796km/h); initial climb (A) 3,100ft (945m)/min, (B) 2,920ft (890m)/min; service ceiling, 41,600ft (12,68km); range with maximum payload of (A, 70,847lb/32,136kg) 4,080 miles (6,565km), (B, 90,880lb/41,222kg) 2,935 miles (4,725km); takeoff to 50ft (15m) (B) 5,800ft (1,768m).

Armament: None.

History: First flight 17 December 1953; service delivery 19 October 1964; first flight of C-141B, 24 March 1977.

Development: In the late 1950s MATS (now MAC) anticipated a severe future shortage of long-range airlift capacity, the C-133 being an interim propeller aircraft and the much larger C-132 being cancelled. As interim solutions orders were placed for the C-135 jet and for a long-range version of the C-130, but on 4 May 1960 a requirement was issued for a purpose-designed transport which was won by Lockheed's Model 300 submission in March 1961. Ordered at once as the C-141, it followed the lines of the C-130, and even had the same 10ft x 9ft (3.1 x 2.77m) body cross-section (a choice which perhaps proved erroneous, as from the start the internal cube volume was totally inadequate for the available weightlifting ability). The C-141 was, in other respects, much larger, with a wing of almost twice the area, swept at only 23° (¼-chord) for good field length but resulting in lower speeds than equivalent civil transports. Features included a full-section ramp/door, side paratroop doors, upper-surface roll/airbrake spoilers, four reversers, tape instruments, an all-weather landing system and advanced loading and positioning systems for pallets and other loads. ▶

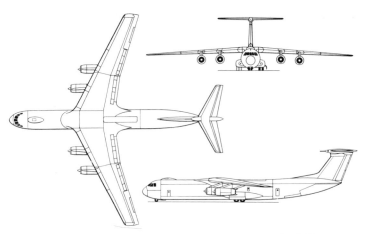

Above: Three-view of the new model, the stretched C-141B.

Above: Takeoff by a C-141A of the 438th MAW, based at McGuire AFB, New Jersey, in the 21st AF. Outstanding in most respects, the C-141 design erred in adhering to the same fuselage cross-section as the C-130, resulting in a basic inability to accommodate the loads it could otherwise lift. This has been rectified in the lengthened C-141B, though the width/height problems still remain.

Left: Arrival in Japan of a C-141A then serving with the 60th MAW.

The first five C-141As were ordered in August 1961, at which time the requirement was for 132 aircraft, but following extremely rapid development and service introduction further orders were placed for a total of 285. Several of the first block were structurally modified to improve the ability of the floor to support the skids of a containerized Minuteman ICBM, a weight of 86,207lb (30,103kg). One of these aircraft set a world record in parachuting a single mass of 70,195lb (31,840kg). Standard loads included 10 regular 463L cargo pallets, 154 troops, 123 paratroops or 80 litter (stretcher) patients plus 16 medical attendants. Usable volume was 5,290 cu ft (150m^3), not including the ramp. Service experience proved exemplary and in the Vietnam war C-141s, many of them specially equipped for medical missions and flown with extraordinary skill to ensure a smooth ride even through severe weather, maintained essentially a daily schedule on a 10,000-mile (16,000km) trip with full loads both ways.

It was this full-load experience which finally drove home the lesson that the C-141 could use more cubic capacity. Lockheed devised a cost/effective

Below: The first of three M-113 amphibious armoured carriers of the US Army emerges from an unmodified C-141A in the 1970s.

This StarLifter, at the time designated as the YC-141B, was the first of MAC's 271 aircraft of this type to be 'stretched'. The bulge aft of the cockpit is the UARRSI (Universal Aerial Refuelling Receptacle Slipway Installation).

U.S. AIR FORCE

stretch which adds 'plugs' ahead of and behind the wing which extend the usable length by 23ft 4in (7.11m), increasing the usable volume (including the ramp) to 11,399cu ft (322.71m^3). The extended aircraft, designated C-141B, carriers 13 pallets or much larger numbers of personnel. It also incorporates an improved wing/body fairing which reduces drag and fuel burn per unit distance flown, while among other modifications the most prominent is a dorsal bulge aft of the flight deck housing a universal (boom or drogue) flight-refuelling receptacle. The first conversion, the YC-141B, was so successful that the Air Force decided to have Lockheed rework all the surviving aircraft (277), to give in effect the airlift ability of 90 additional aircraft with no extra fuel consumption.

All the A models should have been converted soon after this book appears in 1982, the likely total being not 277 but 274. They are assigned to the following MAWs: 60th at Travis, California; 63rd at Norton, California; 437th at Charleston, S Carolina; 438th at McGuire, NJ; 443rd at Altus, Oklahoma; and to part of the 314th TAW at Little Rock, Arkansas.

Below: As noted in the text, a C-141 once held the world record for a heavy-dropped load. Here pallets leave a C-141B in late 1980.

Lockheed SR-71

SR-71A, B and C

Origin: Lockheed-California Company, Burbank, California.

Type: A, strategic reconnaissance; B, C, trainer.

Powerplant: Two 32,500lb (14,742kg) thrust Pratt & Whitney J58-1 (JT11D-20B) continuous-bleed afterburning turbojets.

Dimensions: Span 55ft 7in (16.94m); length 107ft 5in (32.74m); wing area 1,800sq ft (167.2m²).

Weights: Empty, not disclosed, but about 65,000lb (29.5t), loaded 170,000lb (77,112kg).

Performance: Maximum speed (also maximum cruising speed), about 2,100mph (3,380km/h) at over 60,000ft (18,29m); world record speed over 15/25km course, 2,193mph (3,530km/h), Mach 3.31); maximum sustained height (also world record), 85,069ft (25,929m); range at 78,740ft (24km) at 1,983mph (3191km/h, Mach 3) on internal fuel, 2,982 miles (4,800km); corresponding endurance, 1h 30min; endurance at loiter speed, up to 7h.

Armament: None.

History: First flight (A-11) 26 April 1962; (SR-71A) 22 December 1964; service delivery, January 1966.

Development: Unbelievably, Lockheed and the Air Force succeeded in designing, building and completing the flight-test programme of these extremely large and noisy aircraft in total secrecy. President Johnson disclosed the existence of the basic A-11 design in February 1964. It was created by Lockheed's Advanced Development Projects team—the so-called Skunk Works—under vice-president C.L. 'Kelly' Johnson in 1959-61 The requirement was for a platform able to succeed the U-2 for clandestine reconnaissance, and as height was no longer sufficient protection, speed ▶

Below: SR-71As used on combat missions over Southeast Asia in 1967-73 still wear a snake emblem on their vertical tails.

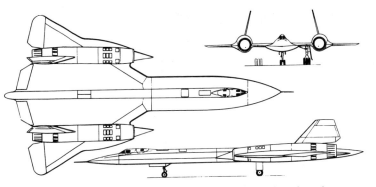

Above: Standard SR-71A with spikes out and nozzles closed.

Above: A Blackbird of the 9th SRW taxis in at Beale after a mission, its braking-parachute doors still open above the body.

U.S. AIR FORCE

had to be added (which in turn translated into still greater height). The engineering problems with the titanium-alloy airframe, the unprecedented propulsion system (which at cruising speed glows orange-white at the rear yeat gets most of its thrust from the inlet) and even the hydraulic system which had to use totally new materials and techniques. Basic features included a modified delta wing with pronounced camber on the outer leading edges, extremely large lifting strakes extended forwards along the body and nacelles, twin inwards-canted pivoted fins above the nacelles, outboard ailerons, inboard elevators and main gears with three wheels side-by-side. The original A-11 shape also featured fixed ventral fins under the rear of the nacelles and a larger hinged central ventral fin.

The first three aircraft (60-6934/6) were built as YF-12A research interceptors, with a pressurized cockpit for a pilot and air interception officer, Hughes ASG-18 pulse-doppler radar, side chines cut back to avoid the radome and provide lateral locations for two IR seekers, and tandem missile bays for (usually) eight AIM-47 AAMs. In 1969-72 two participated in a joint programme with NASA to investigate many aspects of flight at around Mach 3. These aircraft investigated surface finishes other than the normal bluish-black which resulted in the popular name of 'Blackbird' for all aircraft of this family.

It is believed that about 15 aircraft were delivered to the Air Force with a generally similar standard of build, though configured for the reconnaissance/strike role. Designated A-11, they could carry a centreline pod which could be a 1-megaton bomb but was usually a GTD-21 reconnaissance drone looking like a scaled-down single-engined A-11 and with cameras, IR and (variously, according to mission) other sensors in a bay behind the multi-shock centrebody nose inlet. Some dozens of these RPVs were delivered, painted the same heat-reflective black and with similar flight performance (engine has not been disclosed) but with rather shorter endurance. Those not consumed in missions (about 17) were stored at Davis-Monthan.

The A-11/GTD-21 held the fort until, in 1964, the definitive long-range recon/strike RS-71A came into service. (It was announced by President Johnson as the SR-71A and as he was never corrected the 'SR' designation became accepted.) This also can carry a 1-MT bomb pod or GTD-21 or derived RPV, but details of missions and payloads have not been disclosed. With an airframe and increased-capacity fuel system first flown on the fourth ▶

90

Left: The crew disembark from their incredible vehicle as a ground-crewman begins to open one of the inlet-duct doors (still too hot to touch). The SR-71 needs very special ground-support equipment.

Below: The setting sun is reflected off this SR-71A caught by the camera in a rare slow-speed let-down above a thick cloud layer. The aircraft is No 71-7964. The number of SR-71s built has not been disclosed.

Above: The Air Force no longer uses the Lockheed YF-12A, shorter and much lighter (because of smaller fuel capacity) than an SR-71.

▶ A-11 (designated YF-12C) it is longer, has no rear ventrals, optimized forward chines extending to the tip of the nose, and no missile bay but extremely comprehensive and in some cases unique reconnaissance systems for the surveillance of from 60,000 to 80,000 square miles (155,000 to 207,000km²) per hour. The backseater, with a separate clamshell canopy with inserted panes of heat-resistant glass, is the RSO, reconnaissance systems officer. Both crew wear Astronaut suits and follow pre-flight procedures based on those of space missions. The first SR-71A was assigned to a new unit, the 4,200th SRW, at Beale AFB, California, in 1966, which worked up the optimum operating procedures and techniques for best coverage, optimum fuel consumption, minimal signatures and precision navigation, burning special JP-7 fuel topped up in flight by KC-135Q tankers also based at Beale. To facilitate the demanding process of crew conversion to this extremely costly aircraft an operational trainer, the SR-71B, was purchased, at least two being slotted into the main batch of 29

Below: A loose formation with a T-38A emphasizes the impressive size of the SR-71A; this example carries the Vietnam snake badge.

Above: This view of an SR-71 on the landing approach shows the remarkable breadth of the sharp-edged forward fuselage.

Right: Special JP-7 fuel streams from the receptacle of SR-71A No 71-7974 as the boomer in the KC-135Q breaks contact.

(or more) which began at 61-7950. This has a raised instructor cockpit and dual pilot controls, and also includes the reconnaissance systems for RSO training.

After the first crews had qualified as fully operational, in 1971, the parent wing was restyled the 9th SRW, with two squadrons. This has ever since operated in a clandestine manner, rarely more than two aircraft being despatched to any overseas theatre and missions normally being flown by single aircraft. It is not known to what extent subsonic cruise is used; in the normal high-speed regime the skin temperature rises from -49°C to 550/595°C, and the fuel serves as the heat sink and rises to a temperature of about 320°C before reaching the engines, at least one SR-71C was produced as an SR-71A rebuild, following loss of an SR-71B. It has been estimated that the SR-71As seldom fly more than 200 hours per year, mainly on training exercises. No recent estimate has been published of their vulnerability.

Below: Touchdown by an SR-71B trainer, showing both the all-moving canted vertical tails and the 40ft (12.2m) braking parachute.

Lockheed TR-1

U-2A, B, C, CT, D, R, WU-2 family and TR-1A & B.

Origin: Lockheed California Company, Burbank, California.

Powerplant: One Pratt & Whitney unaugmented turbojet, (A and some derivatives) 11,200lb (5,080kg) thurst J57-13A or -37A, (most other U-2) versions) one 17,000lb (7,711kg) thrust J75-13, (TR-1) 17,000lb (7,711kg) J75-13B.

Dimensions: Span (A,B,C,D,CT) 80ft 0in (24,38m), R, WU-2C, TR-1) 103ft 0in (31.39m); length (typical of early versions) 49ft 7in (15.1m), (R, TR) 63ft 0in (19.2m); wing area (early) 565sq ft (52.49m²), (R, TR) 1,000sq ft (92.9m²).

Weights: Empty (A) 9,920lb (4,500kg), (B,C,CT,D) typically 11,700lb (5,305kg), (R) 14,990lb (6,800kg), (TR) about 16,000lb (7,258kg); loaded (A) 14,800lb (6,713kg), (B,C,CT,D, clean) typically 16,000lb (7,258kg), (with 89 US gal wing tanks) 17,270lb (7,833kg), (R) 29,000lb (13,154kg), (TR) 40,000lb (18,144kg).

Performance: Maximum speed (A) 494mph (795km/h), (B,C,CT,D) 528mph (850km/h), (R) about 510mph (8211km/h), (TR) probably about 495mph (797km/h); maximum cruising speed (most) 460mph (740m/h), (TR) 430mph (692km/h); operational ceiling (A) 70,000ft (21.34km), (B,C, CT, D) 85,000ft (25.9km), (R,TR) about 90,000ft (27.43km); maximum range (A) 2,200 miles (3,540km), (B,C,CT,D) 3,000 miles (4,830km), (R) about 3,500 miles (5,833km), (TR) about 4,000 miles (6,437km); endurance on internal fuel (A) 5½ h, (B,C,CT,D) 6½ h, (R) 7½ h, (TR) 12 h.

Armament: None.

Above: Two-seat U-2D at Air Force Flight Test Center, Edwards AFB.

Below: Landing by U-2R No 68-10333, without mission pods.

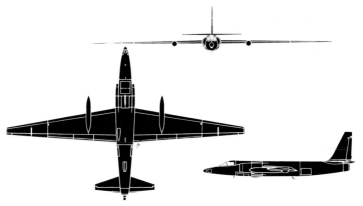

Above: Three-view of original (small) U-2B with slipper tanks.

History: First flight (A) 1 August 1955; service delivery February 1956; operational service, June 1957.

Development: First of the two families of clandestine surveillance aircraft produced by Lockheed's 'Skunk Works' under the brilliant engineering leadership of C.L. 'Kelly' Johnson, the U-2 was conceived in spring 1954 to meet an unannounced joint USAF/CIA requirement for a reconnaissance and research aircraft to cruise at the highest attainable altitudes. The entire programme was cloaked in secrecy, test flying (under Tony LeVier) took ▶

Above: Another of the many rebuilds was this black-painted example, believed to be a U-2L, originally the penultimate U-2B but converted for upper-atmosphere radiation measurements.

▶place at remote Watertown Strip, Nevada, and no announcement was made of delivery to the Air Force of 56-675 and -676, the two prototypes. The original order comprised 48 single-seaters and five tandem-seat aircraft, initially the back-seater being an observer or systems operator. The operating unit was styled Weather Reconnaissance Squadron, Provisional (1st) and soon moved to Atsugi AB, Japan, while the WRS,P (2nd) moved to Wiesbaden, Germany, with basing also at Lakenheath, England. The WRS,P(3rd) remained at Edwards to develop techniques and handle research.

Intense interest in the aircraft, grey and without markings, prompted an announcement that they were NASA research aircraft, with Utility designation U-2, but after numerous unmolested missions over the Soviet Union, China and other territories, one of the CIA aircraft was shot down near Sverdlovsk on 1 May 1960. Future missions were flown by USAF pilots in uniform, with USAF markings on the aircraft. Several more J75-powered aircraft were shot down over China and Cuba, and attrition was also fairly high from accidents, because the U-2 is possibly the most difficult of all modern aircraft to fly. Features include an all-metal airframe of sailplane-like qualities, with a lightly loaded and extremely flexible wing, tandem bicycle landing gears, outrigger twin-wheel units jettisoned on takeoff (the landing tipping on to a downturned wingtip), an unpressurized cockpit with UV-protected sliding canopy of F-104 type, special low-volatility fuel, and large flaps, airbrakes and braking parachute.

From 1959 the J75 engine was installed, and with the U-2C the inlets ▶

Below: Landing a TR-1 is almost as difficult as landing early U-2s.

Above: U-2R No 68-10336 flying with mission containers in place.

Above: One of the original black-painted U-2Bs photographed without pinion tanks over Edwards AFB in 1968. The non-reflective paint then used was to a different specification from that on today's Lockheed TR-1.

Left: The U-2CT is still the type-conversion pilot trainer, used by the 100th SRW at Davis-Monthan AFB.

▶ were splayed out at the front, the U-2D being the original two-seat version and the U-2CT (conversion trainer) being one of at least six rebuilds, in this example as a dual-control pilot trainer with the instructor seated at an upper level. Most CTs have been stationed at the Air Force Flight Test Center and Test Pilot School, both at Edwards. The AFFTC also uses several other versions, including D variants with special instrumentation, dorsal or ventral inlets for sampling, and various external payloads, with a variety of black, white and other paint schemes. Both C and D models have large dorsal 'doghouse' fairings for sampling, sensing or avionic equipment.

Because of high attrition the line was reopened in 1968 with 12 considerably larger aircraft styled U-2R (68-10329 to 10340). While most earlier models could carry 80 US gal (336lit) tanks on the leading edge, the R was supplied with large wing pods permanently installed and accommodating various payloads as well as 105 US gal (398lit) fuel. Wet wings increased internal capacity, and the R also introduced a stretched airframe able to accommodate all necessary fuel and equipment internally. Front and rear main gears were moved closer together and the rear fuselage was formed

Below: A U-2R, No 68-10331, flying almost silently without the mission pods. This, the first of the greatly enlarged variants, introduced a fin platform instead of a dorsal spine.

The first TR-1A single-seater, No 80-1066, seen outside its hangar at Palmdale in July 1981. The TR-1s will be operated by special SAC units on behalf of TAC, the bases being in Europe.

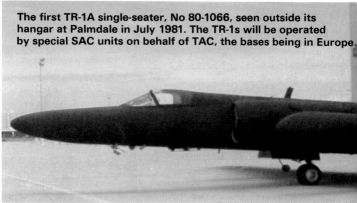

into a bulged upper platform carrying the tailplane. All known U-2R aircraft have been matt black, serving with various overseas commands.

The latest variant, the TR-1, is basically a further updated U-2R with ASARS (advanced Synthetic-Aperture Radar System), in the form of the UPD-X side-looking airborne radar, and with dramatically increased integral-tank fuel capacity, which results in very much higher gross weight. A single-seater, like the R, the TR-1A carries extensive new avionics in its pods, as well as much more comprehensive ECM. Mission equipment is also carried in the nose, in the Q-bay behind the cockpit and between the inlet ducts. Because of the long endurance the Astronaut-suited pilot has special facilities for his personal comfort and for taking warm food. The first batch comprised two TR-1As (80-1061 and 1062) and a third aircraft (1063) which was actually first to be delivered, on 10 June 1981, via the Air Force to NASA with designation ER-2 for earth-rescource missions. Next followed three more TR-1As and a two-seat TR-1B, the eventual fleet expected to number 33 As and two Bs. Main bases will be in Europe, for looking 35 miles (55km) into Communist territory.

Below: Only the expert could tell that this is a U-2R (actually ship 10329) instead of a TR-1. The latter (foot of page) has totally different sensors and more advanced ECM installations.

McDonnell Douglas C-9

C-9A, VC-9A

Origin: Douglas Aircraft Company, Long Beach, California.
Type: Aeromedical airlift transport.
Powerplant: Two 14,500lb (6,577kg) thrust Pratt & Whitney JT8D-9 turbofans.
Dimensions: Span 93ft 5in (28.47m), length 119ft 3½in (36,37m), wing area 1,000.7sq ft (92.97m²).
Weights: Empty about 60,500lb (27,443kg); loaded 108,000 or 121,000lb (48,989 or 54,884kg).
Performance: Maximum speed 583mph (938km/h); maximum cruising speed 564mph (907km/h); initial climb 2,900ft (885m)/min; takeoff field length, 5,530ft (1,685m); range with maximum payload of 22,000lb (9,979kg), about 1,990 miles (3,203km).
Armament: None.
History: First flight (DC-9) 25 February 1955; service delivery 10 August 1968.

Development: While the Navy requested a completely re-engineered DC-9 (as the C-9B Skytrain II) the Air Force bought the DC-9-30 off the shelf, with few modifications as its standard aeromedical transport over tactical ranges. It has three entrances, two with special hydraulic stairways and the third a large door forward on the left side with a hydraulic elevator for loading litters (stretcher patients). Normal loads can be up to 40 litter patients and/or 40 seated, plus two nurses and three aeromedical technicians. There are galleys

Above: Interior of a C-9A Nightingale showing litters and seats.

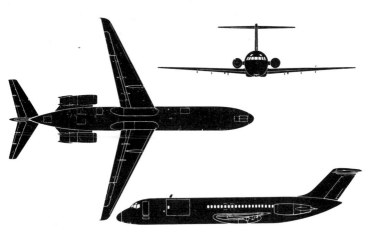

Above: Unlike the Navy C-9B the C-9A has no windows left forward.

and toilets front and rear, as well as a special care compartment with its own environmental controls. A total of 21 C-9As was delivered in 1968-73, equipping the 375th AAW at MAC's headquarters at Scott AFB, Illinois, and the 435th TAW at Rhein Main airport, Germany. The VIP VC-9A (originally VC-9C) force comprises three aircraft assigned to the 89th MAG SAMW at Andrews, near Washington DC.

Above: The first C-9A to be delivered was 67-22583, entering MAC service in August 1968. Curiously, even though it is used in all DC-9 USAF and Navy/Marines versions, and the T-43A, the JT8B engine has never received a military designation.

Left: This Nightingale, No 68-8932, was the first of the second batch. Predictably, this off-the-shelf civil transport (apart from the special interior) has an exemplary record of high-utilization service.

McDonnell Douglas C-17

C-17A

Origin: Douglas Aircraft Company, Long Beach, California.
Type: Long-range heavy airlift transport.
Powerplant: Four 37,600lb (17,055kg) thrust Pratt & Whitney PW2037 turbofans.
Dimensions: Span 165ft 0in (50.29m); length 170ft 8in (52.02m); height 53ft 6in (16.31m); wing area 3,800sq ft (353m²).
Weights: Empty 259,000lb (117,480kg); loaded 572,000lb (259,455kg).
Performance: Normal cruising speed about 495mph (797km/h); takeoff field length with maximum payload, 7,600ft (2,320m); landing field length with max payload, 3,000ft (914m); range with maximum payload, 2,765 miles (4,445km); ferry range 5,755 miles (9,265km).
Armament: None.
History: First flight, possibly 1986; delivery about 1989; full operational capability, 'early 1990s'.

Development: After years of study, which originally centred on tactical aircraft to replace the C-130 (YC-14 and YC-15) but moved to global ranges with the announcement of the Rapid Deployment Force, the USAF was able to issue an RFP for the new C-X long-range heavy airlift transport in October 1980. Douglas's selection was announced in August 1981, but as this book went to press in early 1982 the Air Force had not committed itself to the

programme. The C-17 would be an extremely modern aircraft in all respects, with a 25° supercritical wing carrying four of the newest engines, each with a reverser, blowing back close under the wing to give powered lift when the titanium flaps are lowered. Ground mobility will be exceptional, with four main gears each with a row of three low-pressure tyres, allowing the fully loaded aircraft to turn in an 80ft (24.5m) strip and reverse back up a 2.5% (1 in 40) gradient. The cargo floor would be 87ft (26.5m) long, 216in (5.49m) wide and have headroom of 142in (3.6m) under the wing and 162in (4.1m) elsewhere. Maximum payload would be 172,200lb (78.1t), and apart from an M1 tank (plus other loads) the C-17 could carry wheeled vehicles two-abreast and Jeeps three-abreast. Three electronic displays on the flight deck enable the flight crew to be reduced to two pilots and a loadmaster. The C-17 would combine field mobility at least as good as a C-130 with cargo capability of a C-5A.

In early 1982 the Reagan administration had not ordered the C-17. Instead it is intended to purchase additional KC-10 Extenders and an improved version of the Galaxy, the C-5N (see page 77). In April 1982 McDonnell Douglas did not see the C-17 as entirely dead, however, hoping that the US decision-makers would resume their interest later; but it is unlikely that the aircraft would look exactly as shown below.

Below: Though the four PW2037 turbofan engines would blow into the large flaps, the C-17A would not be such a dedicated STOL (short-takeoff and landing) aircraft as its smaller predecessor the YC-15. This is a McDonnell Douglas artist's impression.

McDonnell Douglas F-4 Phantom II

F-4C, D, E, G and RF-4C

Origin: McDonnell Aircraft Company, St Louis, Missouri.

Type: (C,D,E) all-weather interceptor and attack, (G) EW platform, (RF) reconnaissance.

Powerplant: (C,D,RF) to 17,000lb (7,711kg) thrust General Electric J79-15 afterburning turbojets, (E,G) two 17,900lb (8,120kg) J79-17.

Dimensions: Span 38ft 5in (11.7m); length (C,D) 58ft 3in (17.76m), (E,RF) 63ft 0in (19.2m); wing area 530sq ft (49.2m²).

Weights: Empty (C) about 28,000lb (12.7t), (D) 28,190lb (12,787kg), (E) 30,328lb (13,757kg), (G) about 31,000lb (14.06t), (RF) 29,300lb (13.29t); maximum loaded (C,D,RF) 58,000lb (26.3t), (E,G) 60,360lb (27.5t).

Performance: Maximum speed (C,D,E, Sparrow AAMs only external load) 910mph (1,464km/h, Mach 1.19) at low level, 1,500mph (241km/h, Mach 2.27) over 35,000ft (10.67km); initial climb, low level (AAMs only external load) 28,000ft (8,534m)/min; service ceiling 60,000ft (18.29km) without external stores; range on internal fuel (no external weapons) typically 1,750 miles (2,817km), ferry range (clean except three tanks), (C,D,RF) 2,300 miles (3,700km), (E,G) 2,660 miles (4,281km); takeoff run (clean) 5,000ft (1,525m); landing run 3,000ft (914m).

Armament: (C,D) Up to 16,000lb (7,257kg) assorted stores on external pylons including four AIM-7 Sparrow AAMs recessed into underside of fuselage/wing junction and two more AIM-7, or four AIM-9 Sidewinder, on inboard pylons: (E) same plus 20mm M61A-1 gun under nose; (G) typically three AIM-7 Sparrow recessed, three Mavericks or one Standard ARM plus two AIM-9 on each inboard pylon, and one Shrike on each outboard pylon, plus any other ordnance carried by other versions; (RF) none.

History: First flight (Navy F4H-1) 27 May 1958, (Air Force F-4C) 27 May 1963. ▶

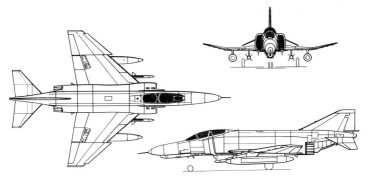

Above: Three-view of an F-4E.

Above: A TAC F-4E in one of the several experimental colour schemes, in this case green, tan and buff (café au lait). This aircraft has its slats open and a Tiseo electro-optical sensor pod on the inboard end of the left-wing leading edge.

Above left: F-4G Advanced Wild Weasels are F-4E rebuilds dedicated to electronic warfare; this one is based at Spangdahlem.

Left: The RF-4C was developed by the Air Force as an unarmed multi-sensor recon platform; this one is from the 1st Tac Recon Sqn at RAF Alconbury.

▶Development: Though it was the result of the manufacturer's initiative rather than an order by a customer, the F4H-11 Phantom II was by a wide margin the most potent fighter of the late 1950s, with outstanding all-round flight performance (resulting in 21 world records), the best radar performance of any Western fighter, the greatest load-carrying capability, and exceptional range and slow-flying qualities to fit it for oceanic operations from carriers. By the early 1960s the Air Force had recognised that it beat even the specialist land-based types at their own missions, and after prolonged study decided to buy the basic F-4B version with minimal changes. The original Air Force designation of F-110 Spectre was changed to F-4C Phantom II under the unified 1962 system, the F-4C being a minumum-change version of the Navy B and preceded (from 24 January 1962) by the loan to TAC of 30 B models ex-Navy.   ▶

Right: Takeoff of an F-4E of the 51st Composite Wing, Osan AB, South Korea, with ALQ-101 ECM pod and Sidewinders. Parked are F-4Ds.

Above: An immaculate F-4E from Langley AFB, with TAC badge on the fin and unit badge on the inlet duct. Four AIM-9J are loaded.

Left: One of the older species is this F-4C, the original Air Force version intended as a minimum-change derivative of the Navy F-4B. Without an internal gun, but with an infra-red sensor in a nose fairing, it is shown in overall air-superiority pale grey in the Air National Guard's 171st FIS, Selfridge AFB, Michigan.

▶   After buying 583 F-4Cs with dual controls, a boom receptacle, Dash-15 engines with cartridge starters, larger tyres and increased-capacity brakes, inertial navigation and improved weapon aiming, the Air Force procured 793 of the F-4D model which was tailored to its own land-based missions, with APQ-109 radar, ASG-22 servoed sight, ASQ-91 weapon-release computer for nuclear LABS manoeuvres, improved inertial system and 30-kVA alternators. Visually, many Ds could be distinguished by removal of the AAA-4 IR detector in a pod under the radar, always present on the C. Next came the extremely sophisticated RF-4C multi-sensor reconnaissance aircraft, a major rebuild in a programme which preceded the D by two years and was the first Air Force variant to be authorised. Designed to supplement and then replace the RF-101 family the RF-4C was unarmed but was modified to carry a battery of forward-looking and oblique cameras, IR linescan, SLAR (side-looking airborne radar) and a small forward oblique mapping radar, as well as more than 20 auxiliary fits including photo flash/flare cartridges in the top of the rear fuselage, special ECM and HF shunt aerials built into the fin behind the leading edge on each side. TAC purchased 505 of this model in 1964-73.

All these variants were very heavily engaged in the war in SE Asia in 1966-73, where political rules combined with other problems to reduce their air-combat performance. Prolonged call for an internal gun resulted in the F-4E, which had the most powerful J79 engine to permit the flight performance to be maintained despite adding weight at both ends. In the nose was the new solid-state APQ-120 radar and the M61 gun, slanting down on the ventral centreline with the 6 o'clock firing barrel near-horizontal, and at the rear was a new (No 7) fuel cell giving enhanced range. The first E was delivered to TAC on 3 October 1967, about three months after first flight, and a total of 949 in all were supplied to maintain the F-4 as leading TAC aircraft with an average of 16 wings equipped throughout the period 1967/77. From 1972 all Es were rebuilt with a slatted leading edge, replacing the previous blown droop which permitted much tighter accelerative manoeuvres to be made, especially at high weights, without stall/spin accidents of the kind which had caused many losses in Vietnam.

Above: This F-4E carries various advanced electronic systems for night ground attack, including the Pave Tack pod on the ventral centreline. The stablized head of this pod contains a laser and FLIR (forward-looking infra-red) boresighted together and interfaced with the ARN-101 digital electronics on board the aircraft.

Left: F-4G Advanced Wild Weasel of the 35th TFW, George AFB, California. The camouflage is standard tan/dark green/ medium green, with the unit badge on the inlet duct and TAC badge on the fin.

The final Air Force variant is the F-4G, the standard Advanced Wild Weasel platform replacing the F-105F and G which pioneered Wild Weasel missions in the late 1960s. The name covers all dedicated EW and anti-SAM missions in which specially equipped electronic aircraft hunt down hostile SAM installations (using radar for lock-on, tracking or missile guidance) and destroy them before or during an attack by other friendly aircraft on nearby targets. The F-4G (the same designation was used previously for modified F-4Bs of the Navy) is a rebuild of late-model F-4E (F-4E-42 through -45) fighters, and has almost the same airframe. It is the successor to the EF-4C, two squadrons of which were fielded by TAC from 1968 and which demonstrated excellent performance with a simpler system. In the F-4G the main EW system is the AN/APR-38, which provides very comprehensive radar homing and warning and uses no fewer than 52 special aerials, of which the most obvious are pods facing forward under the nose (replacing the gun) and facing to the rear at the top of the vertical tail. The system is governed by a Texas Instruments reprogrammable software routine which thus keeps up the date on all known hostile emitters. Offensive weapons normally comprise triple AGM-65 EO-guided Mavericks on each inboard pylon plus a Shrike on each outer pylon; alternatively weapons can include the big Standard ARM (Anti-Radiation Missile), AGM-88 HARM (High-speed ARM) or various other precision air/ground weapons. A Westinghouse ALQ-119 jammer pod is fitted in the left front missile recess, the other three recesses carrying Sparrow AAMs for self-protection. Another change is to fit the F-15 type centreline tank which can take 5g when full with 600 US gal (2,271lit). The G total is 116 aircraft.

Today the F-4 is still the most numerous combat aircraft in the Air Force. User units include: TAC, 4th TFW (E) at Seymour-Johnson, N Carolina; 31st TFW (E), Homestead, Florida; 33rd TFW (E), Eglin, Florida; 35th TFW (C,E,G), George, California; 56th TFW (D,E), MacDill, Florida; 57th FIS (E), Keflavik, Iceland; 57th TTW (E), Nellis, Nevada; 58th TTW (C), Luke, Arizona; 67th TRW (RF), Bergstrom, Texas; 347th TFW (E), Moody, Georgia; 363rd TRW (RF), Shaw, S Carolina; and 474th TFW (D), Nellis. USAFE, 10th TRW (RF), Alconbury, England; 26th TRW (RF), Zweibrücken, ▶

▶ Germany; 50th TFW (E), Hahn, Germany; 52nd TFW (E,G), Spangdahlem, Germany; 86th TFW (E), Ramstein, Germany; 401st TFW (C), Torrejon, Spain; and 406th TFT (various), Zaragoza, Spain. Pacaf, 3rd TFW (D), Clark, Philippines; 8th TFW (E), Kunsan, Korea; 18th TFW (C, RF), Kadena, Okinawa; and 51st CW (E), Osan, Korea. Alaska, 21st CW (E), Elmendorf. Afres, 915th TFG (C), Homestead. ANG, 117th TRW (RF), Birmingham, Alabama, 119th FIG (C), Fargo, N Dakota, 122nd TFW (C), Ft Wayne,

Indiana; 123rd TRW (RF), Louisville, Kentucky; 124th TRG (RF), Boise, Idaho; 131st TFW (C), St Louis, Mo; 148th TRG (RF), Duluth, Minnesota; 149th TFG (C), Kelly, Texas; 152nd TRG (RF), Reno, Nevada; 154th CG (C), Hickam, Hawaii; 155th TRG (RF), Meridian, Mississippi; 159th TFG (C), New Orleans, Louisiana; 183rd TFG (C), Springfield, Illinois; 186th TRG (RF), Meridian; 187th TRG (RF), Montgomery, Alabama; and the 191st FIG (D), Selfridge, Michigan.

Left: Recovery of two F-4Es of the 35th TFW at George AFB, with drag chutes deployed. Note that the same wing's F-4Gs (previous page) have the different tail code WW (Wild Weasel ?).

Below: This F-4G is carrying an AGM-45 Shrike, AGM-78 Standard ARM, ALQ-119 ECM pod and the 600-gal F-15 type tank used by this model.

McDonnell Douglas F-15 Eagle

F-15A,B,C,D and E

Origin: McDonnell Aircraft Company, St Louis, Missouri.

Type: Air-superiority fighter with secondary attack role.

Powerplant: Two 23,930lb (10,855kg) thrust Pratt & Whitney F100-100 afterburning turbofans.

Dimensions: Span 42ft 9¾in (13.05m); length (all) 63ft 9in (19.43m); wing area 608sq ft (56.5m²).

Weights: Empty (basic equipped) 28,000lb (12.7t); loaded (interception mission, max internal fuel plus four AIM-7, F-15A) 41,500lb (18,824kg), (C) 44,500lb (20,185kg); maximum with max external load (A) 56,500lb (25,628kg), (C) 68,000lb (30,845kg).

Performance: Maximum speed (over 36,000ft/10 973m with no external load except four AIM-7), 1,653mph (2,660km/h, Mach 2.5); with max external load or at low level, not published; initial climb (clean) over 50,000ft (15.24km)/min, (max wt) 29,000ft (8.8km)/min; service ceiling 65,000ft (19.8km); takeoff run (clean) 900ft (274m); landing run (clean, without brake chute) 2,500ft (762m); ferry range with three external tanks, over 2,878 miles (4,631km), (with Fast packs also) over 3,450 miles (5,560km).

Armament: One 20mm M61A-1 gun with 940 rounds, four AIM-7F (later AMRAAM) fitting against fuselage, four AIM-9L (later Asraam) on flanks of wing pylons, total additional ordnance load 16,000lb (7,257kg) on five stations (two each wing, one centreline).

History: First flight (A) 27 July 1972, (B) 7 July 1973; service delivery (Cat II test) March 1974, (inventory) November 1974.

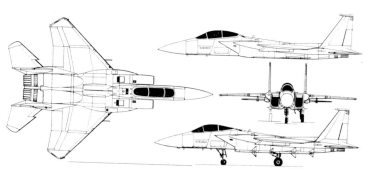

Above: Three-view of F-15A or C with side view (top) of F-15B or D.

Development: Recognizing its urgent need for a superior long-range air-combat fighter the Air Force requested development funds in 1965 and issued an RFP in September 1968 for the FX, the McDonnell proposal being selected in late 1969, with the F100 engine and Hughes APG-63 radar following in 1970. Inevitably the demand for long range resulted in a large aircraft, the wing having to be so large to meet the manoeuvre requirement that it has a fixed leading edge and plain unblown trailing-edge flaps. Two of ▶

Below: There are actually three F-15As in this photograph, which was taken from the back seat of an F-15B. Carrying no missiles except single AIM-9Js, they come from the 58th Tactical Training Wing at Luke AFB, Arizona, which rivals Nellis as a piloting centre.

▶ the extremely powerful engines were needed to achieve the desired ratio of thrust/weight, which near sea level in the clean condition exceeds unity. The inlet ducts form the walls of the broad fuselage, with plain vertical rectangular inlets giving external compression from the forward-raked upper lip and with the entire inlet pivoted at the top and positioned at the optimum angle for each flight regime. The upper wall of the inlet forms a variable ramp, and the lower edge of the fuselage is tailored to snug fitting of the four medium-range AAMs. The gun is in the bulged strake at the root of the right wing, drawing ammunition from a tank inboard of the duct. There is no fuel between the engines but abundant room in the integral-tank inner wing and between the ducts for 11,600lb (5,260kg, 1,739 US gal, 6,592lit), and three 600 US gal (2,270lit) drop tanks can be carried each stressed to 5g manoeuvres when full. Roll is by ailerons, only at low speeds, the dogtoothed slab tailplanes taking over entirely at over Mach 1, together with the twin rudders, which are vertical.

Avionics and flight/weapon control systems are typical of the 1970 period, with a flat-plate scanner pulse-doppler radar, vertical situation display presenting ADI (attitude/director indicator), radar and EO information on one picture, a HUD, INS and central digital computer. In its integral ECM/IFF subsystems the F-15 was far better than most Western fighters, with Loral radar warning (with front/rear aerials on the left fin tip), Northrop ALQ-135 internal counter-measures system, Magnavox EW warning set and Hazeltine APX-76 IFF with Litton reply-evaluator. High-power jammers, however, must still be hung externally, any of various Westinghouse pods normally occupying an outer wing pylon. While the APG-63 offered a fantastic improvement (over any previous Air Force radar) in its ability to track low-level targets, fairly straightforward location of cockpit switches giving a Hotas (Hands on throttle and stick) capability which dramatically improved dogfight performance. Though it was, and remains, concerned at the price, the Air Force got in the F-15A everything it was looking for, and in ▶

Below: 32nd TFW F-15s display their full armament.

Top: Scramble by 32nd TFW F-15 from Camp New Amsterdam.

Above: Dive bombing by F-15B flown solo; heavy loads are possible.

▶1973 announced a force of 729 aircraft including a proportion of tandem dual-control F-15B operational trainers.

Production at St Louis has been running at 90 to 144 aircraft per year, with 675 delivered by the time this book appears. Recipient units began with TAC's 57th TTW at Nellis, 58th TTW at Luke, 1st TFW at Langley, 36th TFW at Bitburg (Germany), 49th TFW at Holloman, 33rd TFW at Eglin, 32nd TFS at Camp New Amsterdam (Netherlands) and 18th TFW at Kadena (Okinawa). Some of these units have received the current production variants, the F-15C and two-seat F-15D. These have a vital electronic modification in a reprogrammable signal processor, giving instant ability to switch from one locked-on target to another, to keep looking whilst already locked to one target, to switch between air and ground targets and, by virtue of an increase in memory from 24K to 96K (96,000 'words'), to go into a high-resolution mode giving the ability to pick one target from a tight formation even at near the limit of radar range. To some extent the latter capability will remain not fully realized until a later medium-range AAM is used (the Air Force has studied the Navy AIM-54 Phoenix but not adopted it). The British Sky Flash would give a major improvement now, especially in severe jamming, but again has not been adopted. The C and D also have 2,000lb (907kg) of additional internal fuel and can carry the Fast (Fuel and sensor, tactical) packs cunningly devised by McDonnell to fit flush along the sides of the fuselage. These actually reduce subsonic drag and offer far less supersonic drag than the drop tanks whilst adding a further 9,750lb

(4,422kg) fuel, or an assortment of sensors (cameras, FLIR, EO, LLTV or laser designator) or a mix of fuel and sensors.

In the second half of 1981 the F-15C re-equipped the 48th FIS at Langley, previously an F-106A unit in now-defunct Adcom, and the Air Force is now procuring aircraft beyond the original 729 force level, partly in order to replace the aged F-106 in CONUS defence. For the future, while one variant of F-15 has been subjected to prolonged study as the USAF's Asat (Anti-satellite) aircraft, firing a large air/space missile based on a SRAM motor followed by an Altair II carrying a nuclear warhead, prolonged testing and demonstration of a company-funded Strike Eagle has now led to the F-15E which may be on order by the time this book appears. This could serve as the Enhanced Tactical Fighter to replace the F-111 (the alternative being the Panavia Tornado) and also as the Advanced Wild Weasel (with far greater capability than the F-4G). The key is the SAR (synthetic-aperture radar) built into the APG-63, which very greatly improves resolution of fine detail against even distant ground targets. With a Pave Tack (FLIR/laser) pod the backseater in the two-seat F-15E can handle what are considered to be the best tactical navigation/target/weapon avionics in the world (apart from the strictly comparable Tornado). External weapon carriage is increased to 24,000lb (10,885kg), including laser-guided and anti-radiation weapons, Harpoon anti-ship missiles, dispensers and other stores. Whether the large existing F-15 force can eventually be brought up to this impressive standard has not been disclosed.

Left: F-15C in current low-visibility two-tone grey. The F-15 has large surface area in relation to its mass.

Below: An F-15A of the 49th TFW, from Holloman AFB, New Mexico, pulls round in a loop.

117

McDonnell Douglas F-101

F-101B

Origin: McDonnell Aircraft Company, St Louis, Missouri.

Type: All-weather interceptor.

Powerplant: Two 14,990lb (6,800kg) thrust Pratt & Whitney J57-55 afterburning turbojets.

Dimensions: Span 39ft 8in (12.09m); length 67ft 4¾in (20.55m); wing area 368sq ft (34.22m²).

Weights: Empty (equipped) 28,000lb (12.7t); loaded (intercept) 39,900lb (19.1t), maximum 46,673lb (21,171kg).

Performance: Maximum speed (40,000ft/18.1km, clean), 1,220mph (1963km/h, Mach 1.85); initial climb, 17,000ft (5,180m)/min; service ceiling, 52,000ft (15.85km); range on internal fuel, 1,550 miles (2,495km).

Armament: Three AIM-4D or AIM-26 Falcon AAMs in internal bay and/or two AIR-2A Genie nuclear rockets externally.

History: First flight (F-101A) 29 September 1954, (B) 27 March 1957; service delivery (B) 18 March 1959.

Development: The original F-101A was intended as a 'penetration fighter' for SAC, but actually went to TAC as an attack aircraft. The F-101B interceptor, one of a series of later variants, differed from all others in having engines with large high-augmentation afterburners, and a second crew-member, accommodated at the expense of reduced fuselage fuel, to manage the MG-13 radar fire-control system tied in with the missile armament. By 1961 the Air Force had received 480 of this version together with the closely related TF-101B dual trainer which retained full armament. At one time 16 Adcom squadrons flew this reliable and well-liked aircraft, but today it is flown only by ANG squadrons assigned via TAC to Norad (and collaborating with similar aircraft flown by; the CAF). Surviving F-101 units are the 107th FIG, Niagara Falls, NY; 142nd FIG, Portland, Oregon; 147th FIG, Ellington AFB, Texas; and the 177th FIG, Atlantic City, NJ.

Above: Three-view of RF-101C with side view (lower) of RF-101G.

Above left: Externally similar to the RF-101G the RF-101H was a rebuild for the Air National Guard of the original unarmed RF-101C reconnaissance version.

Left: The only F-101 model in current operational service is the F-101B all-weather interceptor, still flown with great success by four Air National Guard FIGs. This version is distinguished by its large afterburner nozzles.

119

McDonnell Douglas KC-10

KC-10A

Origin: Douglas Aircraft Company, Long Beach, California.
Type: Air-refuelling tanker and heavy cargo transport.
Powerplant: Three 52,500lb (23,814kg) thrust General Electric F103 (CF6-50C2) turbofans.
Dimensions: Span 165ft 4.4in (50.41m); length 181ft 7in (55.35m); height 58ft 1in (17.7m); wing area 3,958sq ft (367.7m²).
Weights: Empty (tanker role) 240,026lb (108,874kg); maximum loaded 590,000lb (267,620kg).
Performance: Maximum speed (max weight, tanker) about 600mph (9,66km/h) at 25,000ft (7,620m); maximum cruising speed, 555mph (8,93km/h) at 30,000ft (,144m); takeoff field length, 10,400ft (3,170m);

maximum range with maximum cargo load, 4,370 miles (7,032km); maximum range with max internal fuel, 11,500 miles (18,507km); landing speed at max landing weight, 171mph (275km/h).

Armament: None.

History: First flight (DC-10) 29 August 1970, (KC-10A) 12 July 1980.

Development: During the early 1970s the Air Force studied available commercial wide-body transports as a possible ATCA (Advanced Tanker/Cargo Aircraft), and on 19 December 1977 announced the choice of a special version of the DC-10-30CF. The need had been highlighted by the difficulty of airlifting and air-fuelling USAF air units to the Middle East during the 1973 war, when some countries refused the USAF refuelling rights and the KC-135 and supporting cargo force found mission planning extremely ▶

Above and left: The KC-10A Extender is important both to the Air Force and to McDonnell Douglas. Currently no commercial DC-10 is on order for post-1982 delivery and despite the trickle of KC-10A funding the line may have to be closed. The Air Force's decision not to buy the C-17 was a further blow, but this announcement in early 1982 came with the hope of being able to procure 44 KC-10As in addition to the 16 that had been funded at that time. Production at 8 to 10 per year would suffice to keep the line open, and the ultimate force of 60 a real boon to an RDF.

▶difficult. The ATCA was bought to fly global missions not only with several times the overall payload of the KC-135, to a maximum of 169,409lb (76,842kg), but with the ability to provide tanker support to combat units whilst simultaneously carrying spares and support personnel. Compared with the DC-10-30 the KC-10A has a windowless main cabin, with large freight door and five passenger doors, a McDD high-speed boom with fly-by-wire control and able to transfer fuel at 1,500 US gal (5,678lit)/min, and a completely redesigned lower lobe to the fuselage housing seven Goodyear rubberized fabric fuel cells with capacity of about 18,125 US gal (68,610lit). Together with its own fuel the KC-10A has the ability to transfer 200,000lb (90,718kg) to receiver aircraft at a distance of 2,200 miles (3,540km) from home base, and accompany the refuelled aircraft to destination. The cargo floor has improved power rollers and portable winch handling systems, and can accommodate 27 standard USAF Type 463L pallets.

The Air Force hopes eventually to be able to fund 36 KC-10A Extenders, though only at a low rate. In FY79 two aircraft were bought ($148 million, including some engineering costs), in FY80 a total of four, and in FY81 six. The second aircraft (79-0434) was the first to be delivered, to SAC at Barksdale AFB, Louisiana, on 17 March 1981. Ten Extenders will have reached user units by late 1982. There is a possibility that 44 more Extenders will be ordered instead of McDonnell Douglas C-17s.

Above: The centreline gear is prominent in this takeoff picture.

Below: Refuelling trials with a TAC A-10A. The NKC-135A is used for radiation measures by the Aeronautical Systems Division.

Northrop F-5

F-5A Freedom Fighter, F-5B, F-5E Tiger II, F-5F

Origin: Northrop Corporation, Hawthorne, California.
Type: Light tactical fighter.
Powerplant: Two General Electric J85 afterburning turbojets, (A/B) 4,080lb (1,850kg) thrust J85-13 or -13A, (E/F) 5,000lb (2,270kg) thrust -21A.
Dimensions: Span (A/B) 25ft 3in (7.7m) (A/B over tip tanks) 25ft 10in (7.87m), (E/F) 26ft 8in (8.13m), (E/F over AAMs) 27ft 11⁷in (8.53m) length (A) 47ft 2in (14.38m), (B) 46ft 4in (14.12m), (E) 48ft 2in (14.68m), (F) 51ft 7in (15.72m); wing area (A/B) 170sq ft (15.79m²), (E/F) 186sq ft (17.3m²).
Weights: Empty (A) 8,085lb (3,667kg), (B) 8,361lb (73,792kg), (E) 9,683lb (4,392kg), (F) 10,567lb (4,793kg); max loaded (A) 20,576lb (9,333kg), (B) 20,116lb (9,124kg), (E) 24,676lb) (11,193kg), (F) 25,225lb (11,442kg).
Performance: Maximum speed at 36,000ft (11km), (A) 925mph (1,489km/h, Mach 1.4), (B) 886mph (1,425km/h, Mach 1.34), (E) 1,077mph (1,734km/h, Mach 1.63), (F) 1,011mph (1,628km/h, Mach 1.53); typical cruising speed 562mph (904km/h, Mach 0.85); initial clumb (A/B) 28,700ft (8,750m)/min, (E) 34,500ft (100,516m)/min, (F) 32,890ft (1,025m)/min; service ceiling (all) about 51,000ft (15.54km); combat radius with max weapon load and allowances, (A, hi-lo-hi) 215 miles (346km), (E, lo-lo-lo) 138 miles (222km); range with max fuel (all hi, tanks dropped, with reserves) (A) 1,565 miles (2,518km), (E) 1,779 miles (2,863km).
Armament: (A/B) total military load 6,200lb (2,812kg) including two 20mm M-39 guns and wide variety of underwing stores, plus AIM-9 AAMs for air combat; (E/F) Very wide range of ordnance to total of 7,000lb (3,175kg) not inciuding two (F-5F, one) M-39A2 guns each with 280 rounds and two AIM-9 missiles on tip rails.
History: First flight (N-1,56C) 30 July 1959, (production F-5A) October 1963, (F-5E) 11 August 1972.

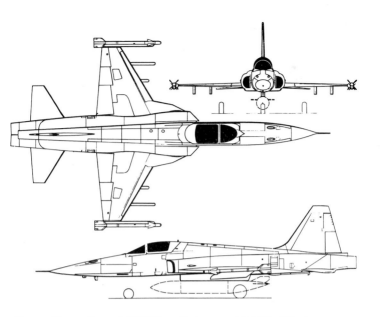

Above: Three-view of F-5E Tiger II; two-seat F-5F is 42in longer.

Development: The Air Force showed almost no interest in Northrop's N-156C Freedom Fighter, which was built with company funds and rolled out in 1959 without US markings. Eventually Northrop secured orders for over 1,000 F-5A and B fighters for foreign customers, and 12 of the MAP ▶

Left: This F-5E is used in the Aggressor role for Dissimilar Air Combat Training at the USAF Fighter Weapons School at Nellis AFB (badge painted on inlet duct).

Above: Another F-5E painted in a Warsaw Pact type colouring, with nose number, this example is from the 527th Tac Ftr Training Sqn at RAF Alconbury, England.

Left: The F-5E Aggressors flight line at Alconbury is constantly busy honing the edge of the sharpest USAF air-combat pilots. Costs are extremely modest.

▶(Mutual Assistance Program) F-5As were evaluated by the Air Force in Vietnam in a project called Skoshi Tiger, which demonstrated the rather limited capability of this light tactical machine, as well as its economy and strong pilot appeal. When the USAF withdrew from SE Asia it left behind many F-5As and Bs, most having been formally transferred to South Vietnam, and few of these remain in the inventory. In contrast the slightly more powerful and generally updated F-5E Tiger II succeeded in winning Air Force support from the start, and the training of foreign recipients was handled mainly by TAC, with ATC assistance. The first service delivery of this version was to TAC's 425th TFS in April 1973. This unit at Williams AFB, Arizona (a detached part of the 58th TTW at Luke), proved the training and combat procedures and also later introduced the longer F which retains both the fire-control system and most fuselage fuel despite the second seat.

Below: An older F-5A making a steep dive-bombing attack, with aiming by the optical gunsight using a manually depressed reticle.

Ultimately the Air Force bought 112 F-5Es, both as tactical fighters and (over half the total) as Aggressor aircraft simulating potential enemy aircraft in DACT (Dissimilar Air Combat Training). About 60 F-5Es and a small number of Fs continue in Air Force service in the development of air-combat techniques, in Aggressor roles, in the monitoring of fighter weapons meets and various hack duties. The F-5Es are painted in at least eight different colour schemes, three of which reproduce Warsaw Pact comouflage schemes while others are low-visibility schemes. The F-5Fs at Williams are silver, with broad yellow bands and vertical tails. User units include the 58th TTW (425th TFS, as described), 57th TTW at Nellis (a major tactical and air combat centre for the entire Air Force), 3rd TFW, Clark AFB, Philippines (Pacaf), 527th Aggressor TFS, attached to the 10th TRW at RAF Alconbury, England; and various research establishments in Systems Command.

Below: Unusual photograph taken by the pilot of one of a pair of Aggressors F-5Es of the 527th; his partner has AIM-9J missiles.

Above: All four Aggressors colour schemes are seen in this formation of Alconbury F-5Es (no AIM-9s).

Left: This colourful F-5E serves with the 425th Tac Ftr Training Sqn at Luke AFB; it has old AIM-9Bs.

Northrop T-38 Talon

T-38A

Origin: Northrop Corporation, Hawthorne, California.
Type: Advanced trainer.
Powerplant: Two 3,850lb (1,746kg) thrust General Electric J85-5A afterburning turbojets.
Dimensions: Span 25ft 3in (7.7m); length 46ft 4½in (14.1m); wing area 170sq ft (15.79m²).
Weights: Empty 7,200lb (3,266kg); loaded 11,820lb (5,361kg).
Performance: Maximum speed, 858mph (1,381km/h, Mach 1.3) at 36,000ft (11km); maximum cruising speed, 627mph (1,009km/h) at same height; initial climb 33,600ft (10.24km)/min; service ceiling 53,600ft (16.34km); range (max fuel, 20min loiter at 10,000ft/3km) 1,140 miles (1,835km).
Armament: None.
History: First flight (YT-38) 10 April 1959, (T-38A) May 1960; service delivery 17 March 1961.

Development: Throughout the second half of the 1950s Northrop's project team under Welko Gasich studied advanced lightweight fighters of novel design for land and carrier operation, but the first genuine service interest was in the N-156T trainer, a contract for Air Force prototypes being signed in December 1956. Unique in the world, except for the Japanese FST-2, in being designed from the outset as a jet basic trainer with supersonic speed on the level, the T-38 was an attractive lightweight version of contemporary fighters, with twin afterburning engines, extremely small sharp-edged wings, area ruling for reduced transonic drag, inboard powered ailerons and slab tailplanes with slight anhedral. The instructor is seated behind and 10in (0.25m) higher than his pupil, both having rocket-assisted seats. To assist the pilot, yaw and pitch flight-control channels incorporate stability augmenters, and great care was taken in 1959-61 to produce an aircraft that pupils could handle. Strictly classed as a basic pilot trainer, the T-38A nevertheless is an advanced machine to which undergraduate pilots come only after completing their weed-out on the T-41A and their complete piloting course on the T-37A jet. The Air Force procured about 1,114 Talons, of which some 800 remain in inventory service with ATC. Their accident rate of some 0.9/11,2 per 100,000 flight

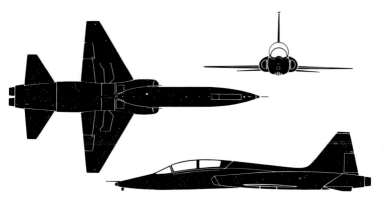

Above: Three-view of T-38A without centreline pod.

hours is half that for the USAF as a whole. An Advanced Squadron of T-38As is based at each ATC school (see Cessna T-37 for list). Many Talons are used as hacks by senior officers, for command liaison and for research, while others are assigned to TAC's 479th TTW at Holloman.

Above: Popularly called the White Rocket, the T-38A has helped 50,000 pilots get their wings. This picture was taken during routine formation training. According to Northrop the T-38 saved taxpayers more than $1 billion because of better-than-predicted safety and maintenance.

Left: Talons equip the USAF Thunderbirds display team, which has found the T-38 easy and economical. Loss of four team-members in January 1982 was tragic, but in no way connected with the aircraft.

Republic F-105 Thunderchief

F105B, D, F and G

Origin: Republic Aviation Corporation (now Fairchild Republic Co), Farmingdale, NY.

Type: (B,D) single-seat fighter/bomber, (F) two-seat operational trainer, (G) EW/ECM platform.

Engine: One Pratt & Whitney J75 two-shaft afterburning turbojet; (B) 23,500lb (10,660kg) J75-5; (D, F, G) 24,500lb (11,113kg) J75-19W.

Dimensions: Span 34ft 11¼in (10.65m); length (B, D) 64ft 3in (19.58m); (F, G) 69ft 7½in (21.21m); height (B, D) 19ft 8in (5.99m), (F, G) 20ft 2in (6.15m).

Weights: Empty (D) 27,500lb (12,474kg); (F, G) 28,393lb (12,879kg); maximum loaded (B) 40,000lb (18,144kg); (D) 52,546lb (23,834kg); (F, G) 54,000lb (24,495kg).

Performance: Maximum speed (B) 1,254mph; (D, F, G) 1,480mph (2,382km/h, Mach 2.25); initial climb (B, D, typical) 34,500ft (10,500m)/min; (F, G) 32,000ft (9,750m)/min; service ceiling (typical) 52,000ft (15,850m); tactical radius with 16 750lb bombs (typical) 230 miles (370km); ferry range with maximum fuel (typical) 2,390 miles (3,846km).

Armament: One 20mm M-61 gun with 1,029 rounds in left side of fuse-lage; internal bay for ordnace load of up to 8,000lb (3,629kg), and five external pylons for additional load of 6,000lb (2,722kg).

History: First flight (YF-105A) 22 October 1955; (production B) 26 May 1956; (D) 9 June 1959; (F) 11 June 1963; final delivery 1965.

Development: The AP-63 project was a private venture by Republic Aviation to follow the F-84. Its primary mission was delivery of nuclear or conventional weapons in all-weathers, with very high speed and long range. Though it had only the stop-gap J57 engine the first Thunderchief exceeded the speed of sound on its first flight, and the B model was soon in production for Tactical Air Command of the USAF. Apart from being the biggest single-seat, single-engine combat aircraft in history, the 105 was notable for its large bomb bay and unique swept-forward engine inlets in the wing roots. Only 75 B were delivered by 600 of the advanced D were built, with Nasarr monopulse radar and doppler navigation. Production was completed with ▶

Above: Three-view of F-105D with three tanks.

Above: Two-seat F-105G Wild Weasel pictured when serving with the 35th TFW at George AFB, California; note Standard ARM missile.

Below: High level bombing by an F-105F doing double duty in the anti-radar role with a white AGM-45A Shrike anti-radiation missile.

▶143 tandem-seat F with full operational equipment and dual controls. The greatest of single-engined combat jets bore a huge burden throughout the Vietnam war. About 350 D were rebuilt during that conflict with the Thunderstrick (T-stick) all-weather blind attack system--a few also being updated to T-stick II--with a large saddleback fairing from cockpit to fin. About 30 F were converted to ECM (electronic countermeasures) attackers, with pilot and observer and Wild Weasel and other radar homing, warning and jamming systems. Westinghouse jammers and Goodyear chaff pods were carried externally. Prolonged harsh use over 20-odd years had by 1982

Below: Already bearing insignia and badges of their new units, these F-105Ds are making a peel-off over March AFB on 11 July 1980 on ceremonial transfer from the 35th TFW to various AFRES and ANG units, in this case mainly to the 108th TFW. Others were in the distance out of the picture. Note differences in centreline payloads.

degraded flight performance of these tough and well-liked aircraft, whose nicknames of Thud, Ultra Hog (the F-84 having been the original Hog and the F-84F the Super Hog) and Lead Sled in no way reflected pilot dissatisfaction with what had been in its day the nearest thing to a one-type air force. In 1982 all had gone from the regular units, survivors being grouped in the Afres 301st TFW at Carswell (flying the B, D and F) and the ANG's 108th TFW (B) at McGuire, NJ; 113th TFW (D), Andrews, Maryland near DC; 116th TFW (G), Dobbins AFB, Georgia; 184th TFTG (F), McConnell AFB, Kansas; and the 192nd TFG (D), Sandston, Virginia.

Below and bottom: Two F-105G Thunderchiefs operating in the dedicated Wild Weasel mode on electronic defence suppression. Missiles are AGM-45 Shrike outboard and AGM-78 Standard ARM inboard. A Westinghouse QRC-380 conformal ECM pod is snug against the fuselage; tanks and dispensers complete the load.

Rockwell B-1

B-1A, B

Origin: Rockwell International, North American Aerospace Operations, El Segundo, California.

Type: Strategic bomber and missile platform.

Powerplant: Four General F101-GE-102 augmented turbofans each rated at 29,900lb (13 563kg) with full afterburner.

Dimensions: (B-1A) Span (fully spread) 136ft 8½in (41.67m), (fully swept, to 67° 30ft) 78ft. 2½in (23.84m); length (including probe) 150ft 2½in (45.78m); wing area (spread, gross) 1,950sq ft (181.2m²).

Weights: Empty (B-1A) about 145,000lb (65,772kg), (B) over 160,000lb (72,576kg); maximum loaded (A) 395,000lb (179,172kg), (B) 477,000lb (216,367kg).

Performance: Maximum speed (B, over 36,000ft/11km) about 1,000mph (1,600km/h, Mach 1.5), (B, 500ft/152m) 750mph (1,205km/h, Mach 0.99); typical high-altitude cruising speed, 620mph (1,000km/h); range with maximum internal fuel, over 7,000 miles (11,265km); field length, less than 4,500ft (1,372m)

Armament: Eight ALCM internal plus 14 external; 24 SRAM internal plus 14 external; 12 B28 or B43 internal plus 8/14 external; 24 B61 or B83 internal plus 14 external; 84 Mk 82 internal plus 44 external (80,000lb, 36,288kg).

History: Original (AMSA) study 1962; contracts for engine and airframe 5 June 1970; first flight 23 December 1974; decision against production June 1977; termination of flight-test programme 30 April 1981; announcement of intention to produce for inventory, September 1981; planned IOC, 1 July 1987.

Development: Subject of a programme whose length in years far outstrips the genesis of any other aircraft, the B-1 was the final outcome of more than

The fourth B-1A (76-0174) represented a standard close to that for the originally planned production aircraft, with inclined fixed inlets, full defensive and offensive electronics (resulting in a blunt tail to the fuselage) and conventional ejection seats.

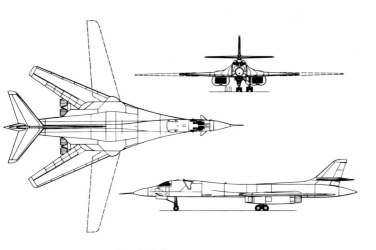

Above: Three-view of early B-1 prototypes.

ten years of study to find a successor to the cancelled B-70 and RS-70 and subsonic in-service B-52. Originally planned as an extremely capable swing-wing aircraft with dash performance over Mach 2, the four prototypes were built with maximum wing sweep of 67° 30ft and were planned to have variable engine inlets and ejectable crew capsules of extremely advanced design. The latter feature was abandoned to save costs, and though the second aircraft reached Mach 2.22 in October 1978 this end of the speed spectrum steadily became of small importance. By 1978 the emphasis was totally on low-level penetration at subsonic speeds with protection deriving ▶

▶entirely from defensive electronics and so-called 'stealth' characteristics. Not very much could be done to reduce radar cross-section, but actual radar signature could be substantially modified, and the effort applied to research and development of bomber defensive electronic systems did not diminish.

The original B-1A featured a blended wing/body shape with the four engines in paired nacelles under the fixed inboard wing immediately outboard of the bogie main gears. Though designed more than ten years ago, the aerodynamics and structure of the B-1 remain highly competitive, and the extremely large and comprehensive defensive electronics systems (managed by AIL Division of Cutler-Hammer under the overall avionics integration of Boeing Aerospace) far surpassed those designed into any other known aircraft, and could not reasonably have been added as post-flight modifications. During prototype construction it was decided to save further costs by dropping the variable engine inlets, which were redesigned to be optimized at the high-subsonic cruise regime. Another problem, as with the B-52, was the increased length of the chosen ALCM, which meant that the original SRAM-size rotary launcher was no longer compatible. The original B-1 was designed with three tandem weapon bays, each able to house many free-fall bombs or one eight-round launcher. Provision was also originally made for external loads. A particular feature was the LARC (Low-

Below: This is believed to be the third prototype, photographed near Edwards AFB in early 1980 soon after application of camouflage.

Altitude Ride Control), an active-control modification which by sensing vertical accelerations due to atmospheric gusts at low level and countering these by deflecting small foreplanes and the bottom rudder section greatly reduced fatigue of crew and airframe during low-level penetration. All four prototypes flew initially from Palmdale and exceeded planned qualities. The third was fitted with the ECM system and DBS (doppler beam-sharpening) ▶

Above: The fourth prototype, escorted by a chase F-111A on one of its last missions in April 1981. Soviet 'Ram-P' is very similar.

Above: Rockwell ground personnel still plugged in to the nose gear as No 4, with camouflaged radome, prepares to leave on one of its last missions in 1981.

►of the main radar, while the fourth had complete offensive and defensive electronics and was almost a production B-1A. The CArter administration decided not to build the B-1 for the inventory, and the four aircraft were stored in flyable condition after completing 1,985.2h in 247 missions.

After further prolonged evaluation against stretched FB-111 proposals the Reagan administration decided in favour of a derived B-1B, and announced in September 1981 the intention to put 100 into the SAC inventory from 1986, with IOC the following year. The B-1B dispenses with further high-altitude dash features, the wing sweep being reduced to about 59° 30ft. As well as refined engines the B-1B can carry much more fuel; a detailed weight-reduction programme reduces empty weight, while gross weight is raised by over 37 tonnes. Main gears are stronger, wing gloves and engine inlets totally redesigned, many parts (ride-control fins, flaps and bomb doors, for example) made of composite material, pneumatic starters with cross-bleed fitted, offensive avionics completely updated (main radar is Westinghouse's APG-66), the ALQ-161 defensive avionics subsystem fitted, RAM (radar-absorbent material) fitted at some 85 locations throughout the airframe, and the whole aircraft nuclear-hardened and given Multiplex wiring. Radar cross-section will be less than one-hundredth that of a B52. Deploying this LRCA.

(Long-Range Combat Aircraft) is intended to bridge the gap until a next-generation 'stealth' aircraft can be fielded towards the end of the century.

Above: Aerial refuelling, here of the third B-1A, extended the duration of test sorties.

Below: Inflight refuelling of one of the early white-painted prototypes in 1977.

Rockwell OV-10 Bronco

OV-10A

Origin: Rockwell International, designed and built at Columbus, Ohio, Division of North American Aircraft Operations (now Columbus plant of NAA Division).

Type: Forward air control.

Powerplant: Two 715ehp Garrett T76-416/417 turboprops.

Dimensions: Span 40ft 0in (12.19m); length 41ft 7in (12.67m); wing area 291sq ft (27.03m²).

Weights: Empty 6,893lb (3,127kg); loaded 9,908lb (4,494kg), overload 14,444lb (6,552kg).

Performance: Maximum speed (sea level, clean) 281mph (452km/h); initial climb (normal weight), 2,600ft (790m)/min; service ceiling, 24,000ft (7,315m); takeoff run (normal weight), 740ft (226m); landing run, same; combat radius (max weapon load, low level, no loiter), 228 miles (367km); ferry range, 1,382 miles (2,224km).

Armament: Carried on five external attachments, one on centreline rated at 1,200lb (544kg) and four rated at 600lb (272kg) on short body sponsons which also house four 7.62mm M60 machine guns with 500 rounds each. ▶

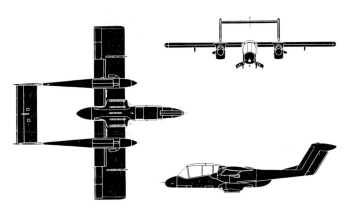

Above: Three-view of standard OV-10A in clean configuration.

Below: An OV-10A, with centreline tank, from the 51st Composite Wing, based at Osan AB, South Korea, part of Pacific Air Forces.

Development: This unique warplane was the chief tangible outcome of
prolonged DoD studies in 1959-65 of Co-In (Counter-Insurgency) aircraft
tailored to the unanticipated needs of so-called brushfire wars using limited
weapons in rough terrain. The Marines issued a LARA (Light Armed Recon
Aircraft) specification, which was won by NAA's NA-300 in August 1964.
Features included superb all-round view for the pilot and observer seated in
tandem ejection seats, STOL rough-strip performance and a rear cargo
compartment usable by five paratroops or two casualties plus attendant. Of
the initial batch of 271 the Air Force took 157 for use in the FAC role,
deploying them immediately in Vietnam. Their ability to respond immediately
with light fire against surface targets proved very valuable, and the OV-10
was always popular and a delight to fly. In 1970 LTV Electrosystems
modified 11 for night-FAC duty with sensors for detecting surface targets
and directing accompanying attack aircraft, but most OV-10s now in use are
of the original model. Units include TAC's 1st SOW at Hurlburt Field, Florida;
the 602nd TACW, Bergstrom AFB, Texas; the 601st TCW, Sembach AB,
Germany; Pacaf's 51st CW, Osan, Korea; and certain specialized schools.

Rockwell T-39 Sabreliner

T-39A, B and F

Origin: North American Aviation (later Rockwell International Sabreliner
Division), El Segundo, California.
Type: (A) pilot proficiency/support, (B) radar trainer, (F) EW trainer.
Powerplant: Two 3,000lb (1,361kg) thrust Pratt & Whitney J60-3
turbojets.
Dimensions: Span 44ft 5in (13.53m); length (original A) 43ft 9in
(13.33m); wing area 342.05sq ft (31.79m²).
Weights: Empty (A) 9,300lb (4,218kg); loaded 17,760lb (8,056kg).
Performance: Maximum speed (A) 595mph (958km/h) at 36,000ft
(11km); typical cruising speed, 460mph (740km/h, Mach 0.7) at 40,000ft
(12.2km); maximum range (A), 1,950 miles (3,138km).
Armament: None.
History: First flight (NA-246 prototype) 16 September 1958, (T-39A) 30
June 1960; service delivery, October 1960.

Development: The Air Force's UTX requirement issued in August 1956
was the first in the world for an executive-jet type aircraft, though at that
time the main mission was expected to be training and utility transport. The
winning design from NAA, which had only the faintest kinship to the Sabre,
was planned with wing-root engines but these were moved to the novel rear-
fuselage position before construction began. The wing was swept and
slatted, and stressed for fighter-type g loads. Rather cramped, the main cabin
had two rounded-triangle windows each side and a door forward on the left
immediately behind the comfortable flight deck. The prototype was put
through Phase II at Edwards only six weeks after first flight, and so
captivated Air Force pilots that seven T-39s were ordered in January 1959.
Ultimately the Air Force bought 149, the majority serving as pilot-
proficiency trainers, utility transports and, in a few cases, as VIP aircraft.
Some spent their lives on research and special trials, the 6th to 9th were
delivered with Nasarr radar to train F-105D pilots (designation T-39B), and
at least three As were substantially modified as T-39F electronic-warfare
trainers, originally for crews of the F-105G Wild Weasel aircraft. Though
usually absent from published lists, almost all the T-39 force remain at work,
many being assigned to combat wings (eg, the 86th TFW at Ramstein,
Germany).

Above: The OV-10A has the capability of carrying almost all light tactical stores, these S. Korean-based examples having rocket pods.

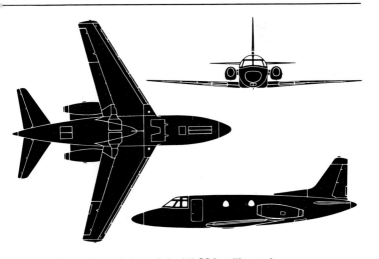

Above: Three-view of the original T-39A utility trainer.

Below: A T-39A in white-top garb; some T-39s are camouflaged.

Vought A-7 Corsair II

A-7D, K

Origin: Vought Corporation, Dallas, Texas.
Type: (D) attack, (K) combat trainer.
Powerplant: One 14,250lb (6,465kg) thrust Allison TF41-1 turbofan.
Dimensions: Span 38ft 9in (11.8m); length (D) 46ft 1½in (14.06m), (K) 48ft 11½in (14.92m); wing area 375sq ft (34.83m).
Weights: Empty (D) 19,781lb (8,972kg); loaded (D) 42,000lb (19,050kg).
Performance: Maximum speed (D, clean, SL), 690mph (1,110km/h), (5,000ft/1,525m, with 12 Mk 82 bombs) 646mph (1,040km/h); tactical radius (with unspecified weapon load at unspecified height), 715 miles (1,151km); ferry range (internal fuel) 2,281 miles (3,671km), (max with external tanks) 2,861 miles (4,604km).
Armament: One 20mm M61A-1 gun with 1,000 rounds, and up to 15,000lb (6,804kg) of all tactical weapons on eight hardpoints (two on fuselage each rated 500lb/227kg, two inboard wing pylons each 2,500lb/1,134kg, four outboard wing pylons each 3,500lb/1,587kg).
History: First flight (Navy A-7A) 27 September 1965, (D) 26 September 1968, (K) January 1981.

Development: The Corsair II was originally derived from the supersonic F-8 Crusader fighter to meet a Navy need for a subsonic tactical attack aircraft with a much heavier bomb load and greater fuel capacity than the A-4. So effective did the A-7 prove that in 1966 it was selected to equip a substantial proportion of TAC wings, and ultimately 457 were acquired. Compared with the Navy aircraft the A-7D introduced a more powerful engine (derived from the Rolls-Royce Spey) with gas-turbine self-starting, a multi-barrel gun, and above all a totally revised avionic system for continuous solution of navigation problems and precision placement of free-fall weapons in all weather. The folding wings and arrester hook were retained, and other features included a strike camera, boom receptacle instead of a probe, boron carbide armour over cockpit and engine, and a McDonnell Douglas Escapac seat. Avionics have been further improved over the years, but the ▶

Below: The prototype A-7K was a rebuilt A-7D, seen here after delivery to the Air National Guard in December 1980.

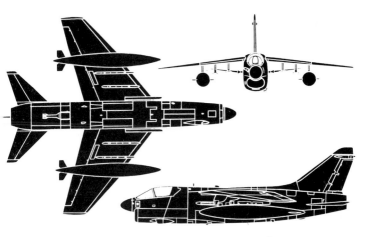

Above: Three-view of A-7D with tanks on outer pylons.

Above: A-7Ds of an unidentified USAF squadron taxiing out on a mission with free-fall bombs. The 20mm M61 guns will be loaded.

▶APQ-126 radar had been retained, programmable to ten operating models, together with British HUD, inertial system, doppler radar, direct-view storage tube for radar or Walleye guidance, and central ASN-91 digital computer. For laser-guided weapons the Pave Penny installation is hung externally in a pod, but the ALR-46(V) digital radar warning system is internal. There is no internal jamming capability, however, and the usual ECM payload is an ALQ-101 or -119 hung in place of part of the bombload. ▶

Below: By 1982 almost all surviving A-7Ds had been passed to the Air National Guard; these are in Colorado (140th TFW, Buckley Field).

Foot of page: Takeoff by a pair of A-7Ds of an Air National Guard unit, with tanks inboard but no bombs. Small and compact, these aircraft can each carry an external weapon load in excess of 15,000lb.

Immediately below: KC-135 boomer's view of an A-7D. The latter appears to carry the mountain lion emblem of the ANG 120th TFS, and thus comes from the same 140th TFW as those on the left. In its day the A-7D set a new high standard of precision bombing accuracy, but in recent years this has been consistently surpassed by the newer-technology F-16.

Production of the A-7D has long been completed, but Vought has recently also delivered 30 of a planned 42 tandem dual-control A-7K Corsairs with full weapons capability. It is planned that 16 will be assigned to the ANG's 162nd TFTG at Tucson, and a pair to each of the 11 ANG's 13 operational units equipped with the A-7D. These units are the 112th TFG, Pittsburgh,

Pennsylvania; 114th TFG, Sioux Falls, Iowa; 121st TFW, Rickenbacker AFB, Ohio; 127th TFW, Selfridge AFB, Michigan; 132nd TFW, Des Moines, Iowa; 138th TFG, Tulsa, Oklahoma; 140th TFW, Buckley, Colorado; 150th TFG, Kirtland AFB, New Mexico; 156th TFG, San Juan, Puerto Rico; 162nd TFG (TFTG), Tucson; 169th TFG, McEntire Field, S Carolina; 178th TFG, Springfield, Ohio; and the 185th TFG, Sioux City, Iowa. In the 1981 Gunsmoke tactical gunnery meet at Nellis the 140th, from Colorado, shot their way to the top team title with an exceptional 8,800 out of 10,000 points (the team chief, Lt-Col Wayne Schultz, winning the Top Gun individual award). The meet involves not only gunnery but bombing and maintenance/loadeo contests. The chief of the judgegs said: 'Some of the scores are phenomenal--pilots are so accurate they don't need high explosive to destroy a target, they are hitting within 1½ to 2 metres, with ordinary free-fall bombs.' Few tactical aircraft are as good at attack on surface targets.

Left: Four of the first definitive A-7Ds (with boom receptacle instead of a probe as on the first 15 aircraft) were assigned to the 57th Fighter Weapons Wing at Nellis AFB.

Below: Snakeye retarded bombs drop from an A-7D of the 23rd Tactical Fighter Wing (England AFB, Louisiana) and slow down violently as their drag-brakes snap open.

Air Weapons

Since its formation in 1948 the USAF has been a world leader in aircraft armament. This section outlines the chief aircraft guns, bombs and missiles at present in use. To these hardware items must be added the electronic software necessary for their delivery, and the ECM and decoys for survival.

Guns

The most important gun used by the Air Force is the General Electric M61A-1, T-171 and related six-barrel rotary cannon in 20mm calibre. This family of guns can be self-powered (GAU-4) but most are driven hydraulically or electrically, with firing rates usually in the region of 4,000 or 6,000 shots/min. Ammunition of various types is drawn from a tank and in all current installation the feed system is linkless (a few link belts are still on charge for F-104s and some contemporary aircraft), and a typical muzzle velocity is 3,400ft (1,036m)/s.

There are many related guns, including the GAU-12/U with five barrels in 25mm calibre which may be adopted in future USAF aircraft. Largest of all guns in this family, and most powerful gun known in any aircraft, the GAU-8/A Avenger has a calibre of 30mm but fires ammunition with more than double the energy of other 30mm guns (except for the Swiss KCA and Russian NR-30, which have about 75% as much kinetic energy per round). This monster gun weighs 3,800lb (1,723kg) and fires from seven barrels in sequence at rates of 2,100 or 4,200 shots/min. It has a hydraulic drive rated at 77hp, and in its sole application, the Fairchild Republic A-10A, is fed by a linkless conveyor from a drum of 1,350 rounds, each roughly the size of a milk bottle. At the opposite end of the scale is the rifle (7.62mm) calibre M134 Minigun, firing at various rates to 6,000spm and used (now only in much-reduced numbers) in fixed, manually aimed and pod installations.

Small numbers of less sophisticated guns are in use. The famed 0.5-calibre (12.7mm) Browning is no longer in service, but the 20mm M-39 with

Above: The most important guns in the Air Force are the 'Gatling' weapons of 20-mm size, such as the M61A-1 under the nose of this F-4E.

Above: By far the hardest-hitting gun in any air force is the GAU-8 of the A-10A; here ammo is loaded at the 354th TFW.

revolving chamber feed survives in a few early F-5s and even in the F-5E (two guns) and F-5F (one). A small number of aircraft, including the OV-10, use the Army M60 7.62mm machine gun. For the future the Air Force has a number of possible guns including the CHAG (Compact High-Performance Aerial Gun) of 30mm calibre, for which competing prototypes are on test by Ford Aerospace (two barrels, 260lb/118kg, 2,000spm) and GE (three barrels, 280lb/127kg, 2,500spm). Various guns using careless ammunition have been tested (one was designed for the F-15 but not selected) and there are high hopes for guns using liquid propellants instead of regular cartridges.

Bombs

There are many hundreds of free-fall ordnance packages either in Air Force service or available. Though large numbers of earlier M-numbered bombs are still on charge, virtually all held at TAC and similar units are of the low-drag type, the most numerous being the Mk 82 of nominal 500lb but actually having a mass around 580lb (262kg). Mk 82 Mod 1 is the same bomb with the Snakeye high-drag tail retarder. The equivalent 250lb (113kg) stores are Mk 81 and Mk 81 Mod 1, while the 2,000-pounder (907kg) is the Mk 83. The commonest 3,000lb (1,361kg) bomb is the older-series M118E2. Nuclear free-fall bombs include the B28 (tactical and strategic versions); the widely used B43, with at least five different yields and carried by such differing aircraft as the B-52 (four), A-7 (four), F-16 (two) and FB-111 (six); the B57 and B61 tactical bombs, and the TX-61. In place of the ▶

▶cancelled B77 the newest nuclear bomb in advanced development is an updated B43 designated B43Y-1 which has the FuFo (full-fuzing option) and free-fall or retarded aerodynamics together with a lifting-aerofoil parachute and setting for airburst or groundburst. The first FAE (fuel/air explosive) bomb was the BLU-76, to which other types such as HSF-1 and -2 are being added. Cluster bombs are very numerous, dispensing HE, fragmentation, incendiary, gas, anti-armour and other kinds of bomblet; designators include prefixes CBU for cluster bomb unit, BLU for bomb live unit and SUU for suspended underwing unit. (Some SUU loads are gun pods, notably SUU-16A and -23A housing M61-type cannon.) ▶

Above: Powered hoist at the 354th TFW loads a Mk 83 (bomb, low-drag, 1,000-lb) on to an A-10A, which lacks precision aiming for it.

Left: One of the most capable military aircraft ever built, the Strike Eagle (here toting cluster bombs) may be ordered as the F-15E.

Below: Hold the page diagonally to see the angle of this attack by an F-4E with free-fall Mk 83s (a Paveway nose is also visible).

Air/surface missiles

▶There is no clear distinction between an air-to-surface missile and a guided or 'smart' bomb. Oldest missile in this category, AGM-12 Bullpup, is seldom seen in front-line units. A radio-command missile, it comes in two sizes (250 and 1,000lb warhead, 113 or 454kg) with packaged liquid rocket propulsion. Another mature weapon is AGM-62A Walleye I, a free-fall bomb with wings (but no motor) with an 850lb (385kg) warhead and guidance by radio command, but having the crucial difference that, instead of the operator in the aircraft having to keep tracking flares lined up with the target, he watches a screen giving a TV picture of the target as seen by a vidicon camera in the nose of the missile. In theory this gives near-perfect guidance, the accuracy increasing as the target is approached, instead of falling off with increasing range. Walleye II is larger, with a 1,565lb (709kg) warhead, but is rare in the Air Force. Numerically the top Air Force ASM, Maverick is a smaller tactical missile developed by Hughes Aircraft and initially issued in AGM-65A form with a solid motor, 130lb (59kg) warhead and self-homing TV guidance. The missile camera can be locked on the target before launch, so this missile can be launched by single-seat aircraft which can leave the scene immediately the missile has fired. The Air Force had 19,000 of these handy rounds, followed by 7,000 AGM-65B Scene-Magnification models in which the missile could be locked-on to a target scene as a clear and much-enlarged image in the cockpit, even if invisible to the pilot. AGM-65C has laser homing, with individual coding so that each missile responds to just one friendly laser designator (in the air or aimed at the target by friendly troops). AGM-65D, not yet (early 1982) in service, has IIR (imaging infra-red) guidance and can be slaved to a laser pod, FLIR or the APR-38 radar warning set carried in the F-4G. It is hoped the IIR Maverick will be worth its high cost because—especially in rainy and misty weather conditions prevalent in Central Europe—it can be locked-on at more than double the range of previous versions or other tactical missiles. Even AGM-65A can in theory be ▶

Right top: Most numerous precision-guided air/surface missile is the Hughes AGM-65A Maverick, here seen on an A-7D.

Right: This A-7 (of the Navy) carries AGM-88A Harm (high-speed anti-radar missile) inboard and AGM-45 Shrike (same mission) outboard.

Below: This F-111 is one of the first to carry the Pave Tack target designator; the missile is a GBU-15 of CWW type.

Below: Dive attack with one of the Paveway series (on Mk 84 bomb) of LGB (laser-guided bomb) missiles, dropped from an F-15.

155

▶effective without the aircraft coming closer to its target than 14 miles (22.5km).

Dedicated anti-radar missiles include Shrike, Standard ARM and Harm. Shrike was the first such missile in use, and it was derived from the AIM-7 Sparrow AAM. With a range of around 18 miles (29km) it could be tuned to known hostile emissions and left to home automatically on the source. Early Shrikes in Vietnam suffered from many problems and were largely ineffective, but those still in use are vastly superior. Standard ARM (AGM-78B) is a much bigger weapon based on the ship-to-air Standard missile and having a launch weight of some 1,400lb (635kg), and range of up to 35 miles (56km) to a powerful emitter. The Mod 1 missile is compatible with the F-4G's APR-38 system; it is not known whether the delayed AGM-78C, D and D-2 (all with significant improvements) have at last been funded to production. Latest anti-radar missile, AGM-88A Harm (High-speed anti-radiation missile) looks like a larger edition of Shrike, this being partly to house a motor of tremendous power which is hoped to accelerate the missile to such a speed that it will strike home before the target radar can be switched off. Launch weight is about 809lb (367kg), but Harm is not expected to be used at ranges greater than 12 miles (19km).

Smart weapons in the recent past have included a wide variety of Paveway and Hobos (Homing Bomb System) missiles, all comprising regular conventional bombs fitted with a homing head and flight controls. In the Air Force the Paveway laser-homing seeker has been adapted to steer the Mk 82 and 84 bombs, the M117 (750lb/340kg) and M118 (3,000lb/1,361kg) and Mk 20 Mod 2 Rockeye family of cluster bombs. Hobos has been used most commonly with the Mk 84 or M118 bombs and has flown guided by EO seekers or, less often, TV or IR. This series of smart bombs led to the GBU-15 and -15(V) series with greater stand-off performance gained through the

Above: Though called a Short-Range Attack Missile the AGM-69A (here carried by FB-111A) can fly ranges up to some 100 miles (160km).

Below: This artist's impression shows an ASALM (Advanced Strategic Air-Launched Missile) fired by a B-1. This project is slipping.

Above: A Mk 84-based Hobos (homing bomb system) with electro-optical guidance. Launch weight is 2,240lb (1,016kg).

use of large wings, either of the planar (variable-sweep) type or as a cruciform of four wings. The two families were thus called PWW and CWW for planar-wing weapon and cruciform-wing weapon. PWWs have demonstrated impressive ranges from B-52 and other aircraft, but since 1980 the CWW has been seen far more often, and can be carried by most Air Force tactical bomber and attack aircraft. The usual size has a 2,000lb (907kg) payload and weighs about 2,617lb (1,187kg).

There are also two strategic missiles carried by aircraft of SAC. AGM-69A SRAM (Short-Range Attack Missile) is a neat wingless dart-like round weighing 2,230lb (1,012kg) and able to carry a W-69 (200-kT) warhead at highly supersonic speed at treetop height or over any other pre-programmed flight path, if necessary making feints and violent changes in course or height, before striking a target up to 105 miles (169km) from the point of release. It is used by the B-52G and H as a defence-suppression missile, and about 1,200 ageing SRAMs remain available. The improved AGM-69B was fully developed but cancelled in 1976. A very different and much slower weapon, ALCM (Air-Launched Cruise Missile) is fractionally larger but in the B-52G and B-1B can be carried in similar numbers (20 in the old bomber, 30 in the future one). Made by Boeing as the AGM-86B, the ALCM is dropped up to 1,550 miles (2,495km) from its target, immediately spreading its swept wings and lighting up its small turbojet engine. This missile entered production in 1981 and was due to achieve IOC with B-52G squadrons in late 1982. The Air Force hopes to procure at least 2,300 ALCMs for air launch. ▶

Below: Launch of a production AGM-86B ALCM from a B-52G of SAC.

Air-to-air missiles

▶Apart from Falcon and Genie, expected to be withdrawn from service soon, the Air Force has only two AAMs, both very old in conception (and originally developed by the Navy) but kept up to date by a long series of improvements. AIM-9 Sidewinder is a short-range missile; AIM-7 Sparrow is classed as medium-range. All versions of Sidewinder in use have IR homing guidance effected by a small seeker head driving four control fins near the front of the 5in (127mm) diameter tubular body. Though large numbers of earlier versions remain in use, most front-line USAF aircraft today carry the greatly improved AIM-9J family, with part-solid-state electronics and detachable double-delta control fins, or the much better still AIM-9L with control fins of greater span and pointed tips, a totally new guidance system and an annular blast/frag warhead triggered by an annular proximity fuze with a ring of eight miniature lasers. The range of early AIM-9s was little more than 2 miles (3.2km), but AIM-9L can be used effectively over ranges up to 11 miles (18km). This approaches the range of early models of AIM-7 Sparrow, which is much larger and has semi-active radar homing guidance. Signals from the CW (continuous-wave) fighter radar illuminate the target aircraft, and the missile aerial inside its nose radome senses the reflections from the target and steers the missile towards their source by means of four large hydraulically driven delta wings at mid-length along the body. Again, though many older versions are in use, the current production model is a much-improved missile, designated AIM-7F. Solid-stage guidance is so compact in the 7F that the warhead has been moved ahead of the wings, making room for a much longer motor which increases the maximum effective range from 25/28 miles to 62 miles (100km). Not many Air Force aircraft can carry AIM-7, the main fighters being the F-15 and F-4, though Sparrow has been fired from the F-16A and it would not be a major task to make the two fully compatible. Despite the British Sky Flash, a very much improved AIM-7 serving with the RAF and Sweden and with performance of a wholly new order in severe clutter or jamming conditions, or against low-level targets, this missile has not been adopted by the Air Force which instead hopes to deploy an AMRAAM (Advanced Medium-Range AAM) later in the decade. This missile, and the parallel ASRAAM (short-range) are in budget trouble, but are intended to replace AIM-7 and AIM-9 before 1987.

Below: The third AMRAAM (Advanced Medium-Range AAM) was test-fired from an F-16 in late 1981. It may replace AIM-7Sparrow.

Above: Back in 1977 a prototype F-16 fired AIM-7F Sparrow missiles, which are not normally carried by these aircraft.

Above: Distinguished by its blunt double-delta control surfaces, the AIM-9J Sidewinder was replaced in production by the AIM-9L.

OTHER SUPER-VALUE AVIATION GUIDES IN THIS SERIES......

OTHER ILLUSTRATED MILITARY GUIDES NOW AVAILABLE...

Modern Fighters and Attack Aircraft
Modern Submarines
Modern Tanks
Bombers of World War II
Modern Warships
Pistols and Revolvers
Rifles and Sub-Machine Guns
World War II Tanks

* Each has 160 fact-filled pages (except civil airliners: 280 pages)
* Each is colourfully illustrated with hundreds of action photographs and technical drawings
* Each contains concisely presented data and accurate descriptions of major international weapons
* Each represents tremendous value

Further titles in this series are in preparation
Your military library will be incomplete without them.

PRINTED IN BELGIUM BY

INTERNATIONAL BOOK PRODUCTION